GIFT
PACKAGING
DESIGN

DESIGN MEDIA PUBLISHING LIMITED

CONTENTS

PREFACE

The basic purpose of packaging undoubtedly lies in its functionality, which protects the products from impact in the transport even in the selling process and benefits for been taken away.

Well, in addition to the most basic functionality, the largest focus is enhancing the value of commodities and attracting the attention of consumers. Just as people need to wear clothes, which is not just for warming, but also pay attention to the personal characteristics and style to highlight the self-personality. The packaging design could well show the contents and characteristics of the products and by virtue of the visual impression to convey it to the minds of consumers, and thus enhance the competitiveness of products and brands.

In addition to the functional nature of these packaged goods, the gift packaging design particularly emphasizes to show the giver's mind, so that to make the recipient feel the sincerity of the giver, and feel the value of commodities, and happily accept it. Hence, the packaging visual effect will be one of the most direct feelings. As soon as the gift is received, there's no more than a set of recognitions: "so nice!"; "What is this? So cute!";"So special" "How so beautiful?" "I am reluctant to open it". The packaging visual effect is the first step to express the mind of the giver, so that the feelings of sincerity and heart is added and multiplied. The gift box or gift packaging for any products emphasizes on the mind of the giver, so the visual design is seemed to be more important than the packaging functionality.

In the process of packaging design, apart from the functionality, HOHOENGINE always pursues to maximise the value creation of packaging, which emphasizes the process of creative thinking, from simple to complex, and actual production vice visa. Whether the use of green packaging material or getting the balance between customer needs and product value or create a focus point of the characteristics in the product, HOHOENGINE tries to show their more cultural ambition.

In addition to the emphasis on the shape of the structure, they also want to integrate more historical and cultural material or human life meaning into the visual design. Culture does not necessarily need a serious design techniques to manipulate, the origin core of the design thinking of HOHOENGINE is just like the company name HOHOENGINE, which means machine making laughter or engine for happy. No fun no gain "is the centre of our thinking, not fun, no gain, and no fun is no interest. Usually, our design works will be hidden in a little interesting elements, like Kenner Park dream box" (Kanner's dream box) aims to let everyone to know about the autistic children, rather than a dogmatic propaganda or DM to communicate. We designed a game at the bottom of the package box, infusing the symptoms and information on autistic children into the game inside, letting the recipient enjoying the desserts made by autistic children to understand them by virtue of playing the game.

We hope that the gift packaging design could add value to the products and encourage consumers to buy and to convey the full gift-giving mood, making itself to be is not just packaging but an extra product beyond the product. For example, the packaging of Taiwan Centennial Blessing Tea gift set, whose shape likes the Chinese lantern. Even though it is a packaging box for the Taiwan Premium top mountain tea, it may be turned into atmosphere lighting and beautiful lanterns. Another example, the New Year gift box design of the Wu Xing Fortune Cake, it can be changed into New Year couplets and bookmarks as soon as the gift is consumed. Packaging can be re-use, which could relatively reduce the waste and form the concept of green packaging. It is also a double win concept, which benefits the packaging and merchandise mutually, and thus achieving the effect of working together to penetrate.

Amone Hsieh

Design Director
HOHOENGINE CO, LTD.

Summary of Gift Packaging

Definition of Gift Packaging

Gift packaging is the package that refers to the group or individuals in daily life and social activities gift to each other to express feelings, such as wedding gift, birthday gift, festival gift, commercial gift and so on.

People in different regions choose different commodities as gift to send to the presentee, Chinese people are more tend to give foods in the traditional holidays like alcoholic drinks and tobacco himalense and cookies, etc. In western countries, people choose gifts more casual and optional, it perhaps a CD which the recipient likes, a book or a tool box. What successful packaging can do is not only making gifts much better, but also meets the expectations of the giver. Only according to the different countries, different areas, different age, and different levels of consumption crowd, make the packaging more targeted that can make the value of the gift amplified to maximise.

Importance of Gift Packaging

The importance of gift packaging first embodies in the protection of

2

3

gift itself, make it's avoid knock against, wear and tear, damage, etc. Especially when choose the crystal products, glass products, ceramic products or jades as a gift to give others. The outer packaging should choose relatively strong materials, and should set up flexible packaging in the inner part in order to achieve the purpose of shock absorption. It will be perfect if it can set up small fixed items inside the boxes, such as belt, card slot, etc. (Figure1)

Secondly, convey the product information intuitively. Take the 'world's best coffees gift set of coffee' work in this book as an example. This coffee brand has eight different coffee flavours, the designer use the ethnic and regional culture for clues to distinguish these eight flavours. Customers can choose the most suitable coffee taste easily by the packaging. (Figure2,3)

Thirdly, promote emotional communication between people. Buyers to express their respect to the recipient with a fine gift, make the recipient feel the value of the gift, and have satisfaction.

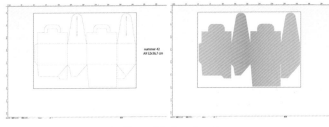

starting with the structure

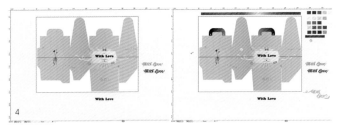

adding the first design elements

The Context of The Creative Thinking When Received Gifts Packing Case

Gift packaging is the packaging design theme that full of human kindness, it has greater flexibility on design processing. In the modeling of packaging that more focus on strong artistic quality, the pursuit of characteristic and the individuality, reflect the giver's personality and culture cultivation, also have good performance on the protection of products and easy to carry.

When do the gifts packaging design, first of all need to choose the materials and packaging design project according to the characteristics of products, match with harmonious colours and patterns, go with the appropriate decorations and so on. Italian designer Romina Iannuzzi shows us her gift packaging design process. (Figure 4,5)

- Make sure the size and do the structural design
- Choose colour
- Design the patterns
- Design ornamental part, such as coloured ribbon, bow, and gift tags etc.
- Packaging products

Two years ago my roommate and I decided to prepare some handmade christmas presents. My goal was to create a kind of little paper bag, with something special inside of it for each person.

First I started by selecting a structure from a packaging book. After that I made the design. Since I love vintage stuff and pastel colours, the result of it was exactly the box you see in the final version. Everything began from a sketch on paper, scanned, traced on Illustrator, and coloured using a Pantone Coated palette. Then I printed out the layout on 300 gr paper, A3 size, together with the tags and the Christmas cards. What followed was to cut and stick, put the Christmas card and the chosen present inside the box, with some wadding to make it seem like snow, close it with a satin ribbon and the tag. Final step: write the name of the person on the tag. Finito!

This project took me two months (October, November), including of course the assemblage of every single piece! I gave 35 boxes to friends, families and office team. Everyone appreciated, I think, and the most of them at first didn't even recognize that the box was handmade.

Romina Iannuzzi

Detail Expressions in Gift Packaging Design

Every gift has its unique significance and characteristic; designers should pay particular attention to explore these items special traits and flash points, and amplify it then make it eye-catching. Such as fragile gifts, need to make the corresponding identification on the packaging. (Figure6)

6

(Figure 7)In order to reflect the original product qualities of this Croatian herbs shop, the designer uses the original gunny bags to express the special traits of the products.

7

Elements of Gift Packaging

1

(Figure1) The Danish designer Stine Engels Henriksen wants to do the packaging design with simply and inexpensive material, he chose common and ordinary kraft paper as the based packaging material, and then use brightly coloured notepaper to creating flowers shapes, that immediately let the packing work looks luxuriantly green, with a happy upward vitality, and looks colourful, extra grace. This is the power what colour bring to a gift packaging, it makes every gift has its own unique character and language.(Figure2) As shown below, the designer uses the bright colour with high saturations to highlight happy and pleasant atmosphere, along with ribbons and gift tags to decorate. That such a beautiful gift, will you not reluctant to open it?

The Pleasant Colour

It is said by Picasso that the colour is same with the form, and it is like peas and carrots with our emotional feelings. Colour is part of the packaging and also become a part of the gift symbol. The colour of packaging material is a kind of suggest that cool colour is clam, warm colour is sweet and happy, red colour represents the mood of hotness and joy, black colour represents grief and sadness, green colour make people feel harmonious and peace as the flavour of natural, and gold colour shows elegance and generous. The white colour reflects the pureness and refinement; however blue colour is full of fantasy and mystery. Therefore, from the colour of the gift packaging, it can decide where the gift is used for.

when designing a gift packaging, the packaging colour should be chosen according to the product's features, cool or warm, light or black, colour purity, and chroma, etc. Colours have great influence on people's mood, and harmonious colours give person implicative, rich, elegant, pleasant and comfortable. Therefore, the collocation of packaging colour can distinguish by age and gender: men mainly use cool colour, women can choose the bright colour or elegant light colour, and children often choose bright colour with lively patterns. (Figure1,2)

Fine Graphics

How to attract consumer's attention effectively among a wide variety of products? This requires the designer make full use of all kinds of ideas and design methods during the packaging graphic design process, to make the packaging image can affect the subconscious rapidly and draw the consumer's attention. Packaging graphics is the main carrier of gift packaging's external information; it can fully display the gift feature and make consumers recognize this gift through the external graphics. The design elements included in gift packaging graphics design are text, illustrations, graphics and patterns, etc. Designer can make full use of these elements to create unique beautiful graphics, in order to convey the characteristics of gifts. The main purpose of gift packaging design is to make gift looks more elegant and more attractive, whether graphics design succeed or not, is the important factor to make the customer interested or be less interested. (Figure3-8)

4

(Figure3) This is a gift bag design for Andreas and Sophia's wedding, white is a symbol of purity of their love, the words on the gift bag are Sophia/Wisdom, Pisti/Faith, Agape/Love and Elpida/Hope, means wisdom, faith, love and hope. This is the theme of their wedding and also the indispensable good quality in marriage life. The designer used these words as the design element for the gift packaging design, to express the blessing to their marriage.

(Figure4) This is an extra virgin olive oil gift box that limit to 1000 in global, box contains three cans of olive oil: one from Portugal, Spain and Italy. Three young art talents from each country illustrated the cans to show different culture and customs of their countries. Each picture illustrates the distinct characteristics of these countries: the great maritime achievements of Portuguese, hot and passionate Spanish lady and luxuriant false face in the Italian Renaissance. The talents illustrated the cans to represent what they love about their countries and dress a beautiful coat for the gift that make people very impressed and could not help collecting these beautiful cans.

5

6

(Figure5,6) This is a set of chocolate packaging design. It has three flavours: orange, lemon and honey. Designer used these taste as a graphic design element skillfully and placed in the slot of the origami leaf divider. So can distinguish the three different flavours-orange, lemon and honey clearly, and the leaves shape external unified packaging didn't destroy the overall harmony. It is environmental friendly since the box is made of recycled paper.

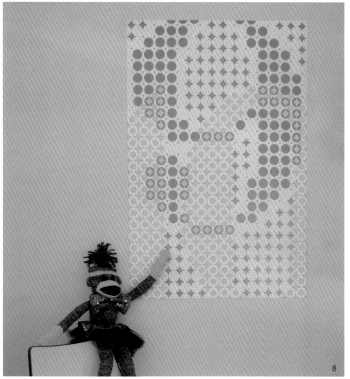

(Figure7,8)This is a gift wrapping paper designed by Studio Kudos for the New Year 2010. Designers use a modest metallic copper colour to represent the past year 2009 and a bright fluorescence green colour to represent the coming year 2010. Designer creates the patterns of basic geometric shapes which are combining of two words. When you look from a distance, you can see the big numbers which represents the year, however, when use them to wrap gift in different size and shapes, it will present patterns of beautiful dot and twinkle stars. Such a beautiful and meaningful gift packaging works show one's own ingenuity and unique.

9

The Design Modeling Element of Gift Packaging

The modeling of gift packaging design is particularly important, and needs to combine handicraft arts with engineering structure design, so it's really a challenge for the designer's aesthetic judgment and practies ability. Excellent gift packaging works should meet the following several requirements. First of all, gift packaging design should give basic protection to the gifts to aviod damage or deformation. Secondly, as a gift it should be convenient to carry and transport. Thirdly, external packaging design must have considerable attractive, should enhance the features and images of the product to catch the customers' attention and impulse the desire to buy, through patterns, texts, colours, shapes and so on. The designer should integrate these requirements, and create the packaging works which can touch customers. (Figure9-11)

10

11

(Figure9) This is a packaging design for Valentine's Day's chocolate. This packaging design is inspired by by James Bond's suitcase in 007 series movies, and it is very convenient to carry. What in the box are secret weapons in the James Bond films, such as a detonating cell phone, X-ray glasses and so on. Of course, these secret weapons are made of chocolate. Is it very cool to carry this box walking in the street? When you open the box to give the chocolate to your beloved and friends, they must be really surprised.

(Figure10) Everyone will love delicious cake. During carry, the cake would usually slide around in the box and the original shape would be destroyed. But you won't have such worry in the packaging design work "sugar". The designer made the bottom of the box in to a taper, then the cake is fixed in the small space of the bottom. And the space in top is large, which ensures the icing is not disturbed, giving it well protection.

(Figure11)This is a very interesting gift packaging design. Designer Shiho Masuda created it into a shirt, and it is vivid and lifelike that can draw your attention at the first sight. So the designer should fully use imagination to create gift packaging which corresponds with the gift's characteristics. For instance, the Valentine's Day's chocolate box, businessmen are more willing to use a heart shape as packaging, meaning to have mutual affinity to expressing love and transfer the romantic feeling. The image of cartoon animal is suitable for expressing fairytales, to transfer cheerful and joy feeling; also the antique modeling is suitable for express the long history, simplicity, reminiscence, etc.

Natural Environmental-friendly Material

*When buying a gift and the seller asks "would you like me to wrap that for you?"
my answer has more and more often been "well...that depends", and only after
seeing what kind of paper and ribbon they use, I would made a decision. For most
people gift wrapping only has a practical purpose, to hide the present inside. But
for me the gift wrapping is a part of the gift and the whole present experience.
Beautiful, stylish, fun, personal and thoughtful gift wrapping isn't just a matter
of buying expensive paper and ribbon – anyone can do that. The dilemma with
wrapping is the fact that it often has a very short life span, and some people will
even rip the wrapping apart in a split second (yes those people do exist!). For me
the real challenge is designing gift wrapping that is exciting, by using inexpensive
materials – best of all recycled materials. That way you will not spend a fortune
on something that is later ripped apart and you can be sure that your wrapping is
even more unique.*

*Once you get an eye for materials you will find that almost anything can be used
for wrapping. I find that if the material has just one good quality you can enhance
that quality and change the rest. For example look at a cardboard box, it might
not look exciting but cardboard has one very good quality, it is rigid and you can
cut it in any shape or form you like. As a gift tag you might cut out a tree shape
and put a hole in it for ribbon. If the colour is boring you can paint it or cut out a
piece of the box that has interesting lettering on it.*

*In one of my wrapping projects I wanted to use some small inexpensive pieces
of notepaper, because I liked the neon colours it had. The pieces were too small
to wrap anything in and the texture was not interesting either, all in all they
had a very cheap feel, but I rolled many pieces into cone shapes and glued them*

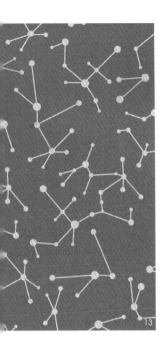

together into big clusters. In this way I enhanced the materials, greatest quality – the colour. (Figure12)

Simple materials don't mean boring wrapping. I love plain brown wrapping paper because it looks great together with almost any material and any colour. Brown wrapping paper is also ideal to draw on, so you don't even need ribbon. Draw patterns, write a joke or poem or draw a face on the present, turning it into a little mascot. If you have kids let them draw on the paper before you use it to wrap your presents. (Figure13,14)

Look at the materials you have at hand, and see it as a challenge to make those materials work. If you don't have enough wrapping paper for your present, then wrap it in two different pieces of paper and make an effect of it. Don't be afraid to reuse wrapping paper either. If it is wrinkled then wrinkle it even more to use it as an effect. And instead of traditional wrapping paper try using materials you would not normally use, for example an old pair of jeans or newspaper with old buttons glued on to it.

Use your imagination and have fun! And as soon as you start to look at gift wrapping as a part of the gift so will the recipient. And you will find that most people will be very touched by the extra effort you have made.

Stine Engels Henriksen

Figurative Design in Gift Packaging

1

The Expression of Givers' Mind

Gift giving itself is used to express feelings, make gift packaging design by oneself also has an emotional appeal. Real hand-making, non-batch production become its unique characteristics, therefore you can tell the receiver loudly that how special this gift it is. (Figure 1) This is a Valentine's Day gift packaging. "TO LOVE" with hand stitching that makes the love feeling like a mild scent comes dispersedly. It has flower seeds in the box, it means that the giver wants to plant the seed of love together and to share the love with you. It is not only implicitly but also romantic. Although the stitches out of the box is not so neat, but it shows sincertity and heart with love of the man who made it. Does anybody will not be touched by such a special gift?

2

Maybe we cannot always find the slap-up and high quality wrapping papers, in fact, a simple kraft paper is enough for packaging. The key is how to processing and decorate it, and let it be shine and luster. We can draw the patterns we like or something that you believe is interesting on the wrapping paper by pastels or highlighters, and then makes a certain format with ribbons and silk ropes. Also we can add some accessories like bows or greeting card according to the needs to decorate the package, and increase the artistic quality through them, bring a finishing touch to the packaging. (Figure 2)

3

4

The Expression of The Receivers' Characteristics

Gift packaging design must take the receivers' characteristics into account, to families, to colleagues or to partners; packaging design should present different styles according to different recipients. For example, the gift which the company giveaway to clients in economic and cultural activities, the purpose is to communicate through the gift and make the clients enhance the good impression of the company and then for the benefit of cooperation. Therefore, packaging visual design need to mainly highlights the enterprise information, such as their logo, name and propaganda messages, in order to enhance the image and influence of the gift-giving company.

If some of the products serve for some specific targets, it must consider

5

6

the specific consumer's interests and hobbies. For example, use children's favorite images and colours for children's products, such as lovely animals, cartoon characters and so on. See the photo of "Kanner's Dream Box" above(Figure5).

Light pink is more suitable for performance gentle feelings of girl, and silk ribbon and lining are expressed their exquisite feelings and precious inner world pertinently. Every girl would really look forward to having a gift with such an exquisite packaging. See the photo of "Two Sweet Boutique" above(Figure6).

(Figure3,4)This is a gift packaging design for O2 Broadband by Irish designer Alan Conlan. There are some small icons of broadband and company logo printed on the box; it is convey the company's information to customers clearly and let them be more impressive about the company.

7

The Expression of Product Image Characteristics

The packaging design style for a product must start from the most significant characteristics of the product itself. In order to enlarge and communicate these characteristics to consumers by way of packaging and make them accept the product and leave a deep impression. The packaging design works by Dan Alexander & Co. design do it very well on that point. (Figure7) As the flagship store of Wissotzky Tea Company, the gift packaging design of "Wissotzky Tea House" conveys the company the characteristics of the products very clearly. (Figure8) It is a very successful case that the pineapple cake packaging designs by Taiwan Victor Branding Design Corp.

(Figure7) The packaging pattern of sailing and ride the wind and waves imply that the tea of Wissotzky comes cross the sea and brings high quality taste pleasure. Word "W" on the sail is the company's logo; it has a simple and clear enterprise information and high brand recognition that make it very easy to accept by the audience.

(Figure8) The designer directly adopts pineapple's appearance as the modeling of packing design, it conveys a clear message that pineapple cake with stuffing of one hundred percent pineapple for people to eat freshly. This product looks vivid and interesting, is absolutely a good gift during the holiday when you meet your relatives and friends.

The Expression of Creative Open Ways

As for the recipient, the most wonderful moment is the expectation and surprise you received when you open the beautiful and colourful coat of a gift. This is a process of expectation and also a process of enjoyment, so the designer can start from this point to give gift packaging another fun.

(Figure9,10) It is a Valentine's Day chocolate packaging, using a lady underwear modeling as the packaging. When the recipient open this gift, it seems to remove pieces of the coat of a beauty. It is a lively and interesting process, also add glorify and beauty to this gift invisibly.

(Figure11,12) Nue Gallery Jewellery Packaging is entirely fixed by the ribbon into the shape of precious stone, the outer packing will be open in a divergence form when loosen the bowknot, it likes the light send out from the jewelry, the real jewelry comes out at that moment.

Form and Style of Gift Packaging

Luxurious Gift Package

According to different levels of gifts, the designer can do the design standing in the point of view of consumers, such as precious wines, jewelry, famous arts and crafts, etc. The high-grade and elegant packaging can improve product's value and artistic value to effectively highlight the characteristics of the expensive products. Can not only reflect the identity of the giver, but also show the giver's accomplishment and high taste. At the same time make the recipient get psychological satisfaction and pleasure.

Regarding this kind of gift packaging the designer should pay attention to the packaging form and the choice of materials. Among many packaging materials, it is very important to choose appropriate materials to reflect gift package of high-grade features. In addition to innovative design concept, the designer also need to know and analyse the structure, function and general processing method of all sorts of materials, in order to reach the best state of packaging design.

(Figure1) The Louis XIII Rare Cask cognac by Rémy Martin is a gift box designed to encase the Louis XIII vintage of Rémy Martin cognac. This gift box, limited edition of 786 bottles in global and each Bottle has its own serial number. It is really expensive that 700 ml sells for 10000 euros, no matter artistic quality and rarity are all belong to the rare. For this kind of rare treasures, there must be match gorgeous and magnificent packaging. Its bottle is use the masterpiece of Baccarat crystal; it shows the precious jewelry quality by its dazzling glory, and bottleneck use very precious palladium decoration. The metal texture outer-package like the armor of ancient warriors; four- petals flowers decorate on the box is originate from the French royal lily sign and more emphasis on RARE CASK is a symbol of French royal unique honor, also shows the symbol of long history and extremely luxury of LOUIS XIII.

2

3

Concise Gift Packaging Design

The simplism, which developed until now, is not only a kind of style trend, but also a life style. Concept of smpleness in design aesthetic arose in the early 20th century. Simplism respire concise design form and make the function above everything. It is the pursuit of a spiritual "essence" regression. Nature and inherent quality is the main idea of simplism.

4

5

6

7

8

(Figure2,3) This is New Year gift packaging designed by BRND WGN for giving their clients. It looks simple but it has hidden beautiful spot. Newspaper is popular packaging materials among young people and fashionistas, it gives a kind of cool and very modern feeling. This newspaper is made by BRND WGN itself, it has some information about the company's information and contact, both reached the propaganda purposes and play the role of the beautification. It is so called kill two birds with one stone.

(Figure4-8) Kiddy´s Class is a children's clothing series products of Zara. As the small gift to children, the designer hopes to be able to use elegant and simple design to attract children's attention. The designer selected recycling recycled paper as the materials, printed lovely monster patterns in the internal side, and hope bring surprise to children when they open it. Are the transparent cartoon pattern stickers which use to be a bag sealing interesting? And there is brand logo on the bag, so that a few simple elements make this gift bag with a very distinct personality.

9

Gift Packaging with Festival Features

Gift packaging are usually used for festival, celebration, wedding, birthday, visiting relatives, regards and so on, it should emphasize its target in the packaging design and reflect the particularity and usage of different kinds of gifts. This requires designers spend full time on the shape, pattern, font and colour during the gift packaging design, and fully express their characteristics.

Red and green are the most common colour in Christmas, of course this cannot exclude the Christmas tree. We can find that is an exquisite Christmas gift through the Figure10. People will naturally think Halloween when they see pumpkins and snow means that the New Year is coming soon.(Figure9,11)

10

11

(Figure9) This is the snowflake wrapping paper designed by Sophia Victoria Joy.
(Figure10) This is the Christmas food box designed by IC4 Design.
(Figure11) This is the Halloween food box designed by IC4 Design.

12

Gift Packaging with The National Characteristics

Today with rapid development of science and technology, gift package will be faced with more wide market. Therefore gift packaging should emphasize design concept, highlight national or local style, and reflect the characteristics with cultural taste. This is a self-evident truth that the more regional and the more national will be more meaningful. People will try to find the most regional souvenirs as a gift to others when they arrive at a strange place. Emphasize traditional culture in gift packaging, inherit the traditional cultural heritage and fully absorb its essence to create the gift packaging with deep national culture, distinctive local characteristics and intense spirit of the times, that will be the excellent gift packaging works.

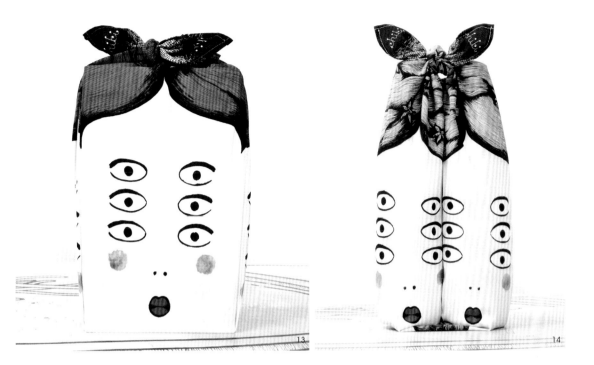

(Figure12) The Wu Xing Fortune Cake designed by Taiwan design company HOHOENGINE is a lunar festival gift box, and this packaging work combined with many traditional Chinese cultural elements, such as traditional pattern, five-element theory, paper-cut art and Spring Festival couplets, etc. It is combined with the green environmental protection demands of modern people, and show you such a nice gift, even a work of art. Its function is also very rich, not only just simple food packaging, but also adhering to the green environmental protection ideas. The whole packaging used recycled paper as its materials, and the body of the box can be cut off as a bookmark and Spring Festival couplets. It may be called a box of multi-purpose and extremely play the role of green recycling.

(Figure13,14) With the continuous development and progress of the society, people are more and more aware of the importance of environmental protection. This packaging design by Italian LL Design Studio was inspired by traditional Japanese packaging culture. Japanese people attach great importance to natural beauty and basically selected natural materials for packaging, such as wood, straw, bamboo, mud, soil, cloth, hemp, paper, etc, using intuitive simpleness to show the sweet, natural of a product. The packaging image is filled with a kind of natural beauty called "unity of man and nature". This work used the simple and beautiful cloth as packaging materials, a kerchief warp up simple goods, which reflect patience and skill to express respect to others. In Japan, the heritage style of art is still visible. Japanese people think that elegant gift packaging is a representative of sincere intention of the giver; it must pay attention to its refinement and beauty. It pursuits the beauty of nature. It is not only a simple packing sheet, but also a shopping bag and even fashion accessories that can be used again.

Bite Me

Designer: Vasily KasSab
Art Director: Vasily KasSab
Client: I'm Health
Date: 2010
Location: UK

The 'BITE ME' brand was developed based on the concept of 'healthy life with correct portions'. Now we can have a correct portion of chocolate since the new packaging is taking into consideration the percentage of cocoa. The more the percentage of cocoa to milk and other ingredients the bigger the chocolate size and vise versa, the less cocoa the smaller the chocolate becomes. Packaging took into consideration distinguishing colours according to different percentages as well, 70%, 80% and 90% as well as small gift chocolate. Shopping bags were customised to suit the boxes. The technique used is 100% ink free, it's a play on the sense of touch, embossing, die cutting and laser engraving was used.

Four Wishes For A Wedding

Designer: Sophia Georgopoulou
Photography: Sophia Georgopoulou, Michalis Kloukinas
Client: Andreas Papadopoulos, Sophia Antoniou
Date: 2011
Location: Greece

Everything started when Andreas and Sophia decided to get married on the name day of the bride, on 17th September (the day when Sophia/Wisdom, Pisti/Faith, Agape/Love and Elpida/Hope are celebrated). The concept of the wedding derives from the particularity of the celebrated day – the four names celebrated on this day could very well be wishes for the couple, for a happy marriage. In Greece, name days are of great importance, similar to birthdays. Thus, an invitation was created in four versions and four different illustrations were created, dedicated to each of the 'wishes'.For the guests giveaway gifts, small paper packages were created containing wedding sugared almonds (traditional Greek sweets, given at weddings).

Monster Box

Design agency: INCH KIEV
Designer: Rezo Gamrekelidze
Photography: Konstantin Stupivtsev
Client: VESNA Workshop
Date: 2011
Location: Ukraine

This candy box is alive! Tiny creature with kind eyes and colourful appearance, its name is Fur-Fur. You can take its hand, touch its ear or just let it stand on its tiny legs, but what's most important - you can open its large mouth and take a candy!

Wissotzky Tea House

Design agency: Dan Alexander & Co.
Designer: Michal Koll
Photography: Ohad Matalon
Client: Wissotzky Tea House
Date: 2008
Location: Israel

It is a project of rebranding the Wissotzky Tea House. The designer defined
its visual language, concept, logo and gift packaging, and positioning the
tea house as the flagship of Wissotzky Tea Company. The visual language
combines a tea-boutique style with the traditional journey of tea blends
across the seas. The company's tea production plant is located in the
industrial area of the Galilee.

Choc on Choc

Design agency: BrandOpus
Designer: Samantha Usborne, Victoria Stoeter
Creative director: Paul Taylor
Client: Choc on Choc
Date: 2009
Location: UK

Choc on Choc, previously named Chocolate on Chocolate, creates unique Belgian chocolate designs using their own patented process to make perfect gifts. The company came to BrandOpus looking for a way to create a more premium look, showcasing the handmade quality of the products through packaging design. The solution reflects the handmade quality nature of the chocolates, with each box featuring a hand-tied satin ribbon and gift tag. These details also add a luxury feel that reinforces the 'gifting' idea behind the products. The brand typeface and stitched effect edge to the packaging also give a handcrafted personality to the brand.

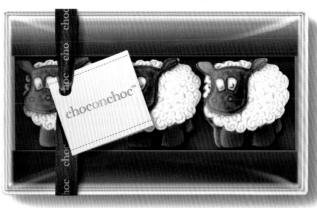

Alt XMAS

Design agency: Alt Group
Designer: Clem Devine, Tony Proffit, Dean Poole
Client: Alt Group
Date: 2010
Location: New Zealand

With the objective of developing an engaging (and edible) Xmas gift for our clients, 150 full size Belgian chocolate keyboards were cast to celebrate Xmas 2010. Some of them may contain traces of nuts. It won Red Dot Award: Communication Design 2011.

Fortune Abalone Australia

Design agency: REB Design
Designer: John Emery, Neil Thomas
Client: Fortune Abalone Australia
Date: 2010
Location: Australia

Abalone is renowned globally as a delicacy worthy of reserve for special occasions. More often than not however, the premium status of the product is poorly reflected in its packaging. With this in mind, Fortune Abalone Australia approached REB Design to manage a branding and packaging programme, which would add value to the produce on offer in its premium retail outlet in Sydney, Australia. The scope of the programme included the development of premium carry bags, proprietary gift packaging for selected dried abalone, and equally elegant packaging for canned produce.

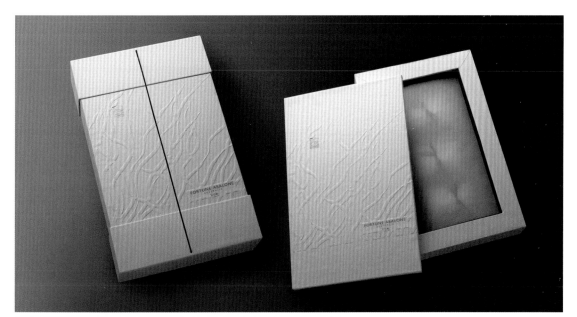

Easter Rabbit(Bunny) Gift Boxes

Design agency: Pixels Plus Paper
Designer: Sam Morris
Client: Pixels Plus Paper online stores
Date: 2010
Location: Australia

These cute Easter Bunny design gift boxes were designed as a result of creative thinking and paper engineering. They are perfect for giving chocolate goodies at a special time of the year-Easter. The front features a bunny face designed with ears that stand up and of course a little tail at the back, and all cut from one single piece of card. They are hand made by Pixels Plus Paper and are available in a range of colours.

Tima & Yui

Design agency: p576
Designer: Arutza Onzaga
Client: Tima&Yui
Date: 2010
Location: Columbia, Bogot

It is brand identity and packaging design for a natural delivery food service.

"World's Best Coffees" Gift Set of Coffee

Design agency: Artemov Artel Graphic Design Bureau
Art directors: Sergii Artemov, Gera Artemova
Designer: Katerina Voytko
Client: Paradise. Gourmet-club™
Date: 2009
Location: Ukraine

'World's best coffees' gift set consist of eight most popular types of coffee in vacuum briquettes. Package was designed to symbolize traveller's suitcase. Simple solution of package allows easily either to demonstrate content in coffee-shops or to transport and present collection. Ethnic and culture motifs of the countries-suppliers of coffee were used in set's package and coffee packs design. Coffee types personification realised using individual stickers with vivid stylized images of ethnic cultures attached to a briquettes surface. Three groups of coffee ('classic', 'exclusive', 'maragogipe') are marked out by specific colour of stickers.

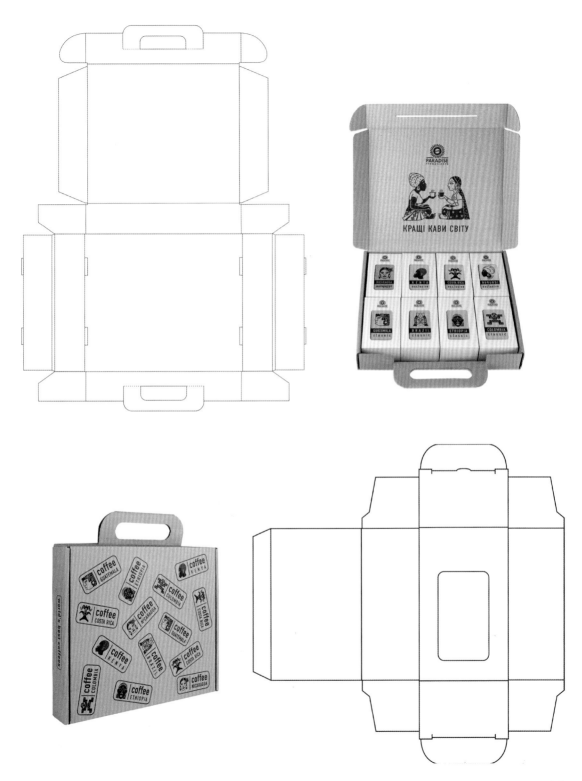

Gift Package for BFS

Design agency: Marin Santic
Designer: Marin Santic
Client: Brac Fini Sapuni
Date: 2011
Location: Croatia

Interweaved of sea, olive oil and healing herbs, Brac Fini Sapuni bears the Mediterranean in their essence. The package is made from white and green coloured paper, carefully chosen to match the visual identity of the brand. It's inner part is folded without glue and gives a very original, unique and natural feeling. The package simplicity goes very well with the colours of the soaps and does not interrupt their design. The illustration on the front shows a renaissance family house in the Postira harbour, housing the first BFS shop on the ground floor.

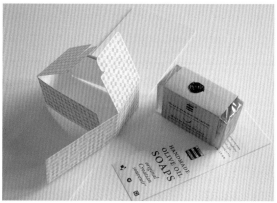

Utai-Cha

Designer: Misako Ishida
Client: personal work
Date: 2010
Location: USA

Utai-Cha Japanese Powder Tea was inspired by the traditional Japanese
tea ceremony. The hand folded origami lid was inspired by the traditional
Japanese clothing, the Kimono.

8-bit Valentine's Day Chocolate

Design agency: Néstor Silvosa
Designer: Néstor Silvosa
Client: Pastelería La Clásica
Date: 2010
Location: Spain

This a work made for the bakery of the designer's neighbourhood called 'La Clásica' (in spanish 'La Clásica' means 'The Classic'). So knowing that in Spain the Valentine's Day is celebrated basically among young people (from teenagers to 40 years old), the designer did a retro design of a chocolate heart made with square chocolates simulating a pixels hearts. By this way, the designer made a tribute to the name of the bakery and the buyers will reminiscing their good old times.

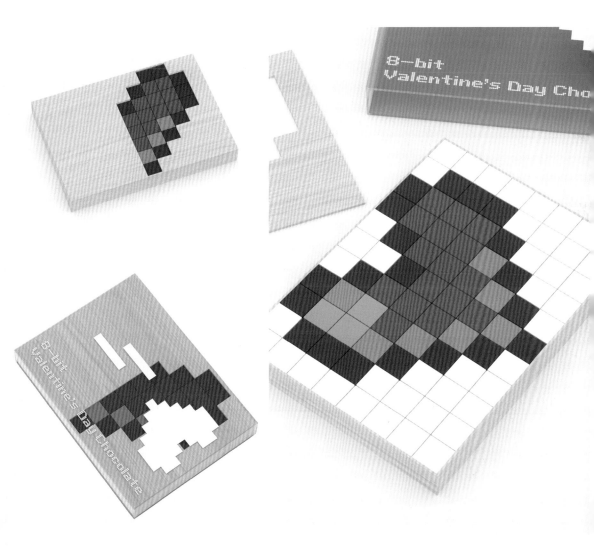

Elemint Chocolate

Designer: Pik Chu Ahmetaj
Client: personal work
Date: 2008
Location: USA

This mint leaf chocolate box is inspired by a gift box. Gift box makes the items look more precious. The mint chocolates in this packaging design, with three flavours: orange, lemon and honey are treated as special jewels and placed in the slot of the origami leaf divider. Each of the boxes is used different graphics on the wrapper placed on top of the box to distinguish the three different flavours-orange, lemon and honey, but the structure of the box helps united the feel of the mint chocolate. By presenting the chocolates in a mint leaf gift box that is for someone special. The box could be reused as gift box. It is environmental friendly since the box is made of recycled paper.

007 Valentine's Day Box

Designer: Jim Sullivan
Art Director: Abby Bennett
Client: Personal Work
Date: 2011
Location: USA

This package design was created as a Valentine's Day gift for the fictional double agent, James Bond of many action packed cinematic thrillers. The box is from Q, his gadget technician. The construction was meant to convey both Bond and Q's relationships and personalities. It seems to be an ordinary briefcase filled with Bond's documents. However, a compartment hidden beneath the documents contains chocolates! Not just any ordinary chocolates, though. These chocolates are shaped to the gadgets from many of the James Bond films, such as a detonating cell phone, X-ray glasses and many more. Close attention to detail in the craft of this piece was the key to its success.

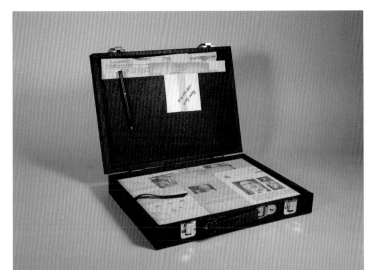

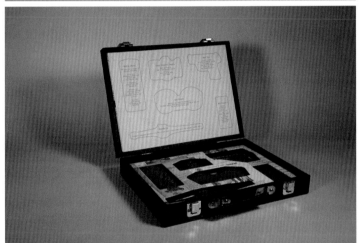

Happy Marmalade Year!

Design agency: MarmeladStudio
Designer: Julia Vyalkina
Client: MarmeladStudio
Date: 2011
Location: Russia

Happy Marmelad Year! This package of marmalade was designed
to wish our colleges, clients and friends a Happy New Year.

HAPPY
MARMELAD
YEAR!

I Love Elassiona

Design agency: Sophia Georgopoulou
Designer: Sophia Georgopoulou
Client: Natsiouli Pelagia
Date: 2011
Location: Greece

For a baby-boy christening ceremony in the city of Elassona (Central Greece), small linen pouches, in brown and light blue colour, were created as baptism giveaway gifts and were given at the end of the christening ceremony. These pouches contained traditional Greek sweets and they were decorated with small cockade pins with various slogans and in a variety of colours. The themes on the cockades were taken from the key cockade of the invitation.

Amelia's Meringues

Design agency: Keri Thornton
Designer: Keri Thornton
Client: Personal work
Date: 2011
Location: USA

Keri Thornton chose to package miniature meringues for the Christmas holiday; due to their delicate, peaked forms which are similar to that of snowflakes. As it was intended that the product was to be given as a gift, the designer decided to make the whole package reusable — with the main structure being a bamboo box that could be kept and reused after consumption. The laser-cut felt embellishment can be hung from the baker's twine, creating a Christmas decoration for the recipients' home. The designer like the idea of the packaging being as enjoyable as the contents, and with the issue of sustainability becoming more prominent, the designer looks for ways to minimise waste, without effecting the beauty of the package itself.

Lavender for BFS

Design agency: Marin Santic
Designer: Marin Santic
Client: Brac Fini Sapuni
Date: 2010
Location: Croatia

Interweaved of sea, olive oil and healing herbs, Brac Fini Sapuni (BFS) bears the Mediterranean in their essence. These natural products made using a traditional family recipe stir up all senses and dazzle you with their tenderness and singlenes. As BFS oppened their first shop on the island of Brac in Croatia they wanted to present more original products from this beautiful island. Considering the tradition of storing lavender bfs packs by themselves using a simple jute bag. With their recognizable red wax seal and paper tag they have created a very original and natural package. Each bag is filled and sealed by hand which gives every bag a unique touch.

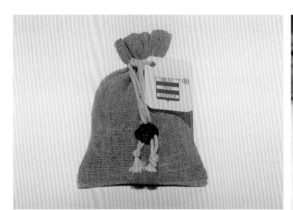

Take it Easy Chocolate Package Design

Designer: Mei Yan Lau
Client: Personal work
Date: 2009
Location: Hong Kong

Chocolate is recognised as a kind of sweets that can bring the feeling of joy and happiness to people, therefore, most of the working people hope for a moment forget the competitive environment, take time off to release the heavy pressure by have a bite of chocolate, this is the original intent of the design. Its background colour is different from the other colourful chocolate packaging, use white as the background colour, and the entire range of design is simple and modern. Each box contains 31 different tastes of chocolate, such as white banana, cappuccino, and each kind of taste has the different pattern designs with the written of encouragement or funny words in order to relieve the bad mood that people suffered from a variety of difficult situations in the company.

31 DAYS.

Merry Tea

Design agency: Studio Kmzero
Designer: Debora Manetti, Francesco Canovaro
Client: personal work
Date: 2011
Location: Italy

How to set some totally hand-made greetings for people you love?
• Buy some different kind of teas (better if you choose cinnamon, almond, sweet orange flowers, etc)
• find some hour of free-time with your partner
• get a Christmas movie like Love Actually or The Holiday
• design a packaging mixing your style and the one of your partner
• melt the butter and the chocolate
• create little pack for all the people you love!

Plant Your Dreams and Let Them Grow

Designer: Sophia Georgopoulou
Client: personal work
Date: 2010
Location: Greece

"Plant Your Dreams and Let Them Grow" is the title of Sophia's Georgopoulou self-initiative project and her wish for 2011! The actual tulip flowers and their 'unique' names (e.g. 'Red Emperor', 'Pink Diamond', 'Sweetheart' etc.) inspired the designer to create a series of ecological and interactive packages containing tulip bulbs. The packages were sent as gifts to friends and clients and offered them a unique experience by telling them to 'Plant Their Dreams', take care of them and see if they will grow (and come true) the following year. The illustrations created on the packs were inspired by the name of each 'unique' tulip and were drawn by hand.

how to plant your dreams:

characteristics:

up to 0.5m ↕   ← up to 0.3m

how to grow them
with success:

needs sun   medium water   cold resistant

Red Emperor   Purissima   Sweetheart

Pink Diamond   Orange Emperor   Candela

Cafe Vue

Design agency: Elise Grace
Designer: Elise Grace Wilken
Client: Cafe Vue
Date: 2010
Location: Australia

It is environmentally sound packaging for macaroons and chocolates. The doily inspired box transforms into a stand to present the delicious French sweets as a great gift for lovers.

SushiSushi

Design agency: Nikki Gittins Design
Designer: Nikki Gittins
Client: personal work
Date: 2011
Location: UK

It is a range of packaging for new Japanese meal for one. The personality packs' structure relate to the traditional individual; Geisha nipped in at the waist, Samurai straight edged, and Sumo budging at the sides.

The packs feature three separate boxes in the style of the traditional Japanese Bento lunchbox to hold different components of the meal; starter, main and condiments.

Taiwan Blessing Seal Cup Set

Design agency: HOHOENGINE CO., LTD.
Designer: Kristy Wen Ho, Amone Hsieh
Client: BONHO INC.
Date: 2011
Location: Taiwan, China

The packaging design use window decoration pattern and seal cutting fonts as the visual focal point. 'Blessing' is the main bless words in Chinese culture, what folk meaning stands by window decoration pattern is not only make our life more beautiful but also where to place our wish for pursuing and keen for the ideal life. Wishes for live in plenty, for the prosperity of offspring, for the land yields good harvests and the people enjoy good health and fortunes to show the old rich cultural connotations behind window decoration patterns. The visual design use four different window decoration patterns as the main parts to represent the blessing, and choose red colour to match the cups. All these are symbols of lucky. Inside of the package use pad, therefore it can put the cups down to present the most featured characteristics - seal cutting in the bottom. A red string linked the up lid and the down one, in order to contain the four separate cups and shows a lantern-shaped appearance with Chinese style, also be continuity in vision with all this series of products. The designer used different printing for each side to make that two kinds of design coexist in one box, meanwhile the package can be reused after take out the cups, and it can transform into a new-year candy box which full of luck with elegant appearance.

Taiwan Centennial Blessing Tea Gift Set

Design agency: Amone Hsieh , Feng-Chung Chen
Designer: Amone Hsieh , Feng-Chung Chen
Client: HongLuBao
Date: 2011
Location: Taiwan, China

The package is surrounded by the four words(FU/LU/SHOU/XI) of blessing. The patterns of these tea gift boxes are reminiscent of traditional imagery used in old Chinese architecture to adorn windows and lampshades. The detailed ornaments symbolise hope, wellness and prosperity as well as the joy of celebrating the 100th anniversary of the founding of Taiwan. The sophisticated packaging concept consists of an inner box, enveloped by an outer sleeve, containing tea leaves as well as cups. Thanks to its decorative patterning, the outer sleeve can also be used as a lantern. The four different coloured boxes are packaged together and can be carried with a delicate loop handle

Wu Xing Fortune Cake

Design agency: HOHOENGINE CO., LTD.
Designer: Feng-Chuan Chen
Client: BONHO INC.
Date: 2010
Location: Taiwan, China

The innovative new-year gift packaging is more than just a box containing
a delicious treat. Inspired by ancient Chinese astrology and Wu Xing which
signifies the five elements, typical Taiwanese design accent and traditional
Chinese New Year custom are blended into this red pentagon shape. Each
side represents one element which also corresponds to animal: Gold –
chicken, Wood – dog, Water – pig, Fire – goat and Earth – cow. In addition,
the package is multipurpose. Concept of traditional Chinese paper cutting
is being applied, so that it can be used also as a display during Chinese
New Year which signifies fortune and luck, and each of the five sides can
be used as bookmarks as luck and fortune surrounds you all year long!

Kanner's Dream Box

Design agency: HOHOENGINE CO., LTD.
Designer: Kristy Wen Ho, Amone Hsieh
Client: Kanner Support Group in Taiwan
Date: 2011
Location: Taiwan, China

Cookies and pineapple cakes in the Kanner's Dream Box is the gift to children, and it proves the best for autistic children's potentials to gain living ability. The slant trapezoid shape of the box symbolizes the stage of a place ground. The lid is covered by a big hearts combined with many cute patterns. Simple lines with rich colours are main elements for those illustrations to show happy animals and children living naturally with joy and independence. It expresses the abundant hope and love in this place. Children patterns with various of Kanner logo signifies as the first step that Kanner children happily start their self-sustain life here.

In addition, the Box is not only a container. The designer specially designs a very interesting and educational board game inside the box. So the recipients can eat and play, savor the desserts and have fun with games at the same time. While finding more usage of the box, the recipients can learn more about Kanners through the special designed game.

Antônio Prendada - Gift Packages

Design agency: Studio Móbi
Designer: Gabriela Andrade
Client: Antônia Prendada
Date: 2011
Location: Brazil

Antônia Prendada is a brand created by a lady who was born and raised in a countryside of Brazil famous for its rooted traditional characteristics. Currently based in a big city, she wants to bring the bucolic atmosphere of the fields and the cultural traditions of the countryside of Minas Gerais to the urban life.

The materials are simple: thread, needles, buttons and fabrics that are transformed into flowers, birds, chickens, cow and other animals, besides the traditional figures found in Brazil. Each product, very kindly handmade, is exclusive and unique. Antônia Prendada is a brand that brings back, revives, and reinvents popular traits of Minas Gerais' culture.

This package set developed for the brand applies simple materials, such as kraft, commonly used for bread bags, without letting go the rustic and handicraft charm raised by traditional characteristics. The gift packs have also a special detail: handcrafted textile tags and sewn lines to seal it up.

Stick Sweets Factory

Design agency: IC4DESIGN
Designer: Hirofumi Kamigaki
Creative Director: Hirofumi Kamigaki, Mari Miyshita
Client: STICK SWEETS FACTORY
Date: 2011
Location: Japan

IC4DEIGN made the packing designs and illustrations for STICK SWEETS FACTORY. The designer made packages which have happy, cheerful and unique feel. They were designed for each seasons and themes. The designer hoped the customers feel happy and joyful with the packages designed.

Festival Gift Bag

Design agency: IC4DESIGN
Designer: Hirofumi Kamigaki
Client: STICK SWEETS FACTORY
Date: 2011
Location: Japan

IC4DEIGN made the packaging designs and illustrations for STICK SWEETS FACTORY. The designer designed these gift bags for each seasons and festivals. The design of bag is casual, stylish and standard. Moreover tags which fit with the festivals are attached with the bag. The designer hopes the customers feel happy when they get the small gift.

The Olive Oil Experience - Limited Ed

Design agency: Guilherme Jardim Packaging
Designer: Guilherme Jardim, Mário Belém, Mar Hernández e Mauro Donatis
Client: Taste Local
Date: 2011
Location: Portugal

TGTL is a food hunting company that aims to present the best gastronomic products the world has to offer. Gift box is limited to 1000 units and it is an exceptional gift for people who are interested in art, design, culture and fine food. Hand packaged box contains three cans of award winning extra virgin olive oil from Portugal, Spain and Italy. Three young art talents from each country illustrated the cans to represent what they love about their countries

Christmas Packaging Chocolate, Traditional

Design agency: Inhouse Studio V&D
Designer: Ilse van der Velde
Client: V&D Warenhuizen bv, Amsterdam, The Netherlands
Date: 2007
Location: The Netherlands

It is a chocolate packaging for Christmas. It has a traditional look, with red and green, because the customer asks for that.

Tarts, Truffles, Rumballs Packaging

Design agency: Designjane Ltd.
Designer: Jane Russo
Client: Coupland's Bakeries
Date: 2010
Location: New Zealand

New graphic elements, package design and colour placement were created to promote Truffles, Tarts and Rum-balls for sale as Christmas gifts, for a New Zealand based Bakery.
Designer Jane was able to simply and effectively promote the 'Kiwi Christmas' theme and ensured packaging was clearly branded for the bakery by;
- Creating New Zealand / Christmas / Holiday themed icons
- Using classic 'brand' elements (Logo, Fonts, Colours)
- Creating a subtle layout to work for various flavours
- Utilising bright colours for impact
- Colour choices to work with and enhance the flavours

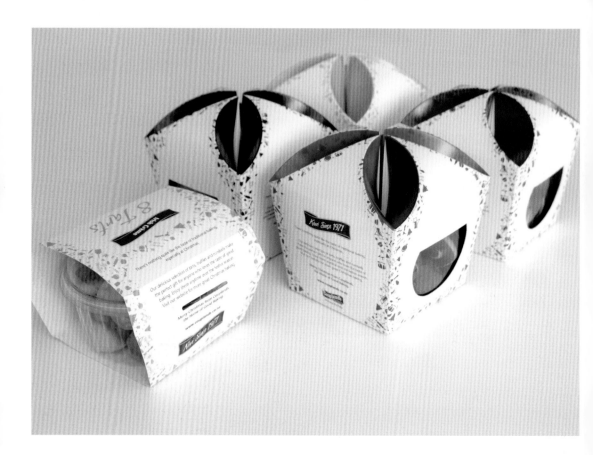

Tea Box

Design agency: Katrine Austgulen
Designer: Katrine Austgulen
Client: Rosehip Tea
Date: 2008
Location: Norway

Tea Box is a rosehip tea box with a fresh retro look that captures the attention among all the traditional tea boxes. The unique opening of the box makes it stand out even more, and separates it from the other brands.

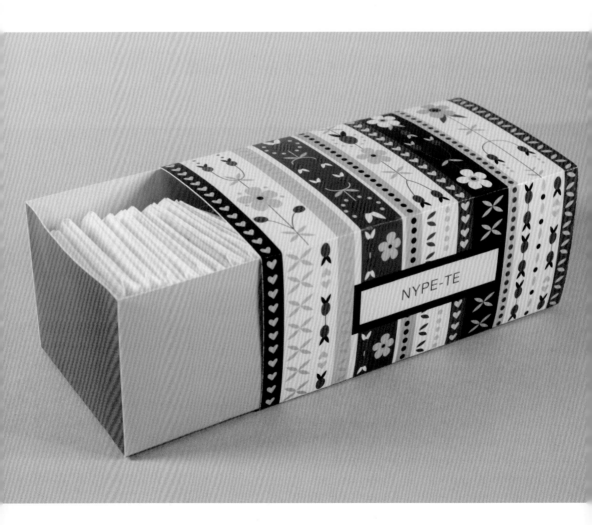

NYPE-TE
P.B. 6329 Etterstad
0604 Oslo
Tlf: 22 88 17 70
www.nypete.no

24 teposer
Innhold: En blanding av soltørkede, viltvoksende
nyper (60%) og vill Hibiscus (40%).
Nettovekt: 84 g.
Holdbarhet: se stempel nederst. I uåpnet pakning og
på tørt sted er Nype-te holdbar i årevis. Etter to år vil
aromaeffekten gradvis bli svakere.

Bra for både deg og miljøet
- Naturlige C-vitaminer.
- Miljøvennlige teposer uten metallstift og snor for å
  unngå unødig emballasje.
- Usprøytede nyper av førsteklasses kvalitet.
- Koffeinfri, for nattesøvnens skyld.

Best før utgangen av: 09.2013
                         L8003

NYPE-TE
P.B. 6329 Etterstad
0604 Oslo
Tlf: 22 88 17 70
www.nypete.no

24 teposer
Innhold: En blanding av soltørkede, viltvoksende
nyper (60%) og vill Hibiscus (40%).
Nettovekt: 84 g.
Holdbarhet: se stempel nederst. I uåpnet pakning og
på tørt sted er Nype-te holdbar i årevis. Etter to år vil
aromaeffekten gradvis bli svakere.

Bra for både deg og miljøet
- Naturlige C-vitaminer.
- Miljøvennlige teposer uten metallstift og snor for å
  unngå unødig emballasje.
- Usprøytede nyper av førsteklasses kvalitet.
- Koffeinfri, for nattesøvnens skyld.

Best før utgangen av: 09.2013
                         L8003

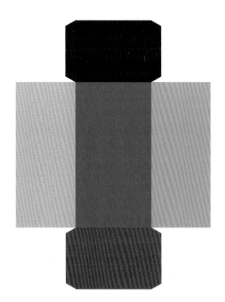

Früute

Design agency: Ferroconcrete
Designer: Owen Gee , Priscilla Jimenez, Ann Kim, Sunjoo Park, Wendy Thai
Creative director: Yo Santosa
Client: Fruute
Date: 2011
Location: USA

Früute is a mini tart shop in West Hollywood, CA, blending gourmet flavour, whimsy and modern design. The menu features classics like tiramisu and crème brulee, and the more curious like wasabi and black pepper chocolate. Früute caters to an upper end market and those wanting to experience something unique. The client wanted a contemporary, minimal and natural feel to the brand, conveying a fresh take on a traditional dessert - the humble fruit tart – elevating its perception to edible art without feeling snobby. The challenge was to find just the right balance in establishing a brand and environment that did not feel too cold or inaccessible, nor too rustic with the use of natural wood materials and simplified brown product packaging. The design of the brand also had to allow the exquisitely beautiful and colourful tarts to come alive and ultimately speak for themselves.

SUSTAINABLE FORESTRY INITIATIVE · Certified Sourcing · www.sfiprogram.org · SFI-01575 · please recycle me

früute

tarts unordinary

Naughty Nibbles

Designer: Alicia Grady
Client:　Personal work
Date: 2009
Location: Australia

Naughty Nibbles was created in response to a brief requiring a brand concept and packaging for Valentine's Day chocolates. The concept, targeted towards females aged 18 to 25 plays with the idea of a strip tease, in which various layers are removed to reveal a sculptured chocolate torso.

Undress your chocolate lov
a delicious Valentine's d

Simply use the tab to strip their clothes
at a time for the ultimate swe

TK. FOOD -Pineapple Cake

Design agency: Victor Branding Design Corp
Designer: Kuo Chung Yang
Client: TK FOOD CO., LTD
Date: 2011
Location: Taiwan, China

The product series directly adopts pineapple's appearance as the modeling of packing design, which means "pineapple cake with stuffing of one hundred percent pineapple for people to eat freshly" and besides emphasizing true pineapple stuffing, the original and innovative packing box design skips the ordinary styles in the market, and it's a must-buy gift.

Salma Hayek Wedding Gift

Design agency: Zoo Studio
Designer: Gerard Calm
Client: Ramon Morató (chocolate artist)
Date: 2009
Location: Spain

Gerard Calm designed a packaging of the gift for the guests at the wedding of
Salma Hayek & François-Henri Pinault.

Re-Interpretating the Mexican Piñata

Design agency: SPECTRO DESIGN STUDIO
Designer: Mariel Alanis, Tere Hinojosa, Mariana Salas
Client: Christmas Gift for SPECTRO clients
Date: 2011
Location: Mexico

This Christmas the designer took on the challenge of investigating and reinterpreting the Mexican piñata with the goal of recreating it into a lovely Christmas present for all the clients. The designer started off with an info graphic card explaining the supposed origins of the piñata and ended up producing very own mini version. Originally the Mexican tradition explains each peak of the piñata as a representation of a capital sin but the designer wanted to give its own meaning. The designer gave each peak what they thought were the best advice or 'tip' for a better working environment and the whole concept was based on the idea of breaking the piñata as a symbol of the breakthrough you'd have at work when following these simple habits. And of course, the designer couldn't forget the candy, symbol of the 'fruits' of a hard work.

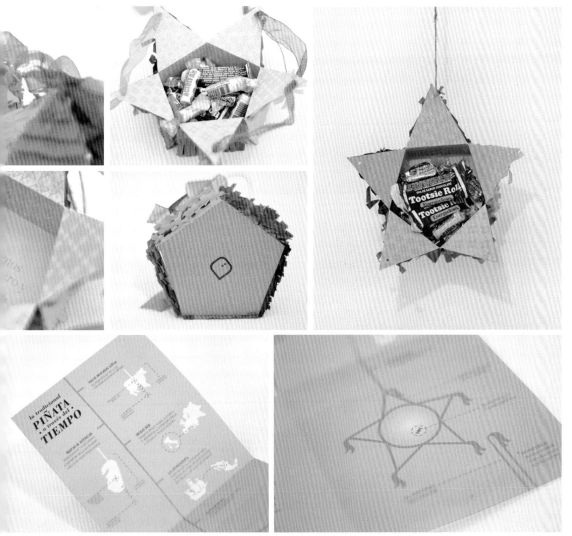

Sugar

Design agency: Savannah College of Art and Design
Designer: Becca Miller
Client: Personal work
Date: 2010
Location: USA

Due to the rise in popularity of gourmet cupcake stores, the designer designed a gourmet cupcake box. Most boxes the designer had encountered at these boutiques were usually white and oversized. During transportation, the cake would usually slide around in the box and destroy the treats initial gorgeous effect. This cupcake box was designed to reinforce the attractiveness of the treat as well as transport the cake safely. The base of the box is purposefully tapered for easy extraction and ensures the icing is not disturbed. The pillowed dome top mimics the icing on the cake and enforces its attractiveness with the decorative paper.

True Rum

Design agency: Zoo Studio
Designer: Gerard Calm
Client: True Rum/Ramon Morató
Date: 2009
Location: Spain

It is concept and gift packaging design for True Rum. The packaging aims to promote the seal of quality True Rum. The pack contains coins made of chocolate and Caribbean rum by the chocolate artist Ramon Morató.

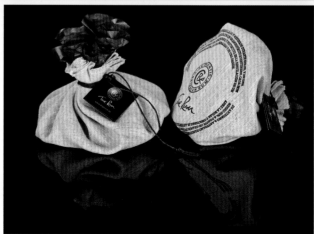

Emptea

Design agency: INCH KIEV
Designer: Rezo Gamrekelidze
Client: VESNA Workshop
Date: 2011
Location: Ukraine

Tea is a very ancient drink, so the agency decided to update its package. This is a convenient and fresh construction, which also fits the shelf in a store. Its special feature is the wayof box opening and closing opens and closes. One box looks like a piece of cake, and six boxes, bound with a ribbon, make a bee's cell that looks very attractive on the shelf and can be easily used as a gift package.

Design agency: Chez Valoises
Designer: Michel Valois
Client: La Face Cachée de la Pomme
Date: 2009
Location: Canada

Chez Valois created special edition discovery gift set packaging for Neige ice ciders. With its mirror-like backing, the set attracts the consumer's attention. This one piece packaging, made with no glue has a complementary tasting note form slide in the back. The cidery La Face Cachée de la Pomme is inspired by the technique used to make ice wine, and by Québec's very particular climate. Neige (meaning snow in English) ice ciders were born out of this Canadian province's terroir which has the extreme cold winter temperatures needed to produce the concentration of sugars for its creation.

Designer: Gina Rodriguez
Client: Personal work
Date: 2010
Location: USA

This wine label was in dire need of a face lift. It was essential to break through all the muddled mess. In this case, the designer was instructed to choose an existing wine company to re-brand. Pahlmeyer is an intimate winery located in Napa Valley, California. The designer favoured this company by reason of seeing this as a great opportunity to re-create an enterprise in which personality was clearly lacking. The designer had to create a conceptual design for two price points, one being a cabernet, and a chardonnay label at a price point of $16, and a premium cabernet, including a gift box, for a price point of $120.

Aalborg Jubilæums Akvavit

Designer: Nicolai Henriksen, Thorbjørn Gudnason,
          Christina Stougaard, Casper Holden
Client: personal work
Date: 2011
Location: Denmark

This product is a celebration of the 100th year anniversary for Aalborg Taffel Akvavit, 1846. The intension with the redesign was to reach a younger target group, while still having the elderly consumers in mind. The designer have made a new label for the new bottle, but kept the current traditional logotype. One of the recognizabilities of this liquor is its taste of oak, which designer chose to highlight. The gift packaging which is handcrafted in oak, will be more expensive in purchase than just the bottle, and will be a preferable luxury choice for anniversary presents.

Vinegar Works Gift Box

Design agency: Design HQ Inc.
Designer: Ian McSorley
Client: Valentine Farm
Date: 2006
Location: Canada

Valentine Farm's Vinegar Works produces several organic wine vinegars from Pinot Meunier and Gewürztraminer grapes. For the product labeling, the designer designed two labels — one for each grape. The four infused flavours were identified with a set of neck labels — black backgrounds for use on the clear bottles and light backgrounds for use on the dark green bottles. As a limited edition promotion, the designer built pine boxes with sliding lids that were the exact fit for a tissue-wrapped bottle. Each box also contained a little eight panel booklet with serving suggestions; recipes and a brief story on the vineyard. Hanging outside the box in a cellophane-wrapped bundle was a weighted pouring spout with our seasonal greeting tag. Kim and John, the Vinegar Works owner/operators liked the package so much that they have sourced a box supplier in Summerland, BC so they can offer the gift box as well as individual bottles.

Eat Drink Merry

Design agency: Alt Group
Designer: Tony Proffit, Aaron Edwards, Dean Poole
Client: Hudson Gavin Martin
Date: 2009
Location: New Zealand

Hudson Gavin Martin is a boutique legal practice formed by three partners, who advise on Intellectual Property and Technology Law in Australasia. Colloquial wisdom has it that all good(and bad) things come in threes. The concept of three is an important part of the Hudson Gavin Martin brand. The gift itself was three bottles of wine; Merlot, Merlot Cabernet and Cabernet Merlot – all the ingredients for a celebration. Each bottle included a set of measures to guide the willing participant through the consumption of its contents and the effect.

Red
Hawkes Bay Merlot Cabernet
2007

Green
Hawkes Bay Merlot
2008

Blue
Hawkes Bay Cabernet Merlot
2009

Seasoned Greetings

Design agency: Alt Group
Designer: Shabnam Shiwan, Aaron Edwards, Dean Poole, Tony Proffit
Client: Northink
Date: 2007
Location: New Zealand

Quack, Crackle, Hop. Christmas is a time of celebration of things that are born in mangers, barns and stables. Just like the Kiwi summer, barbecues and Xmas were meant to go together. For the recipients of this gift, duck, pork and rabbit are this year's seasoned greetings. The process of unwrapping the gift was essential to the design solution. Each wine bottle was paired with a young tasty animal, and revealed instructions for cooking that animal. Quack—Flame grilled duck with fresh summer salsa. Crackle—Best pork fillets with grilled asparagus and spicy spuds. Hop—Skewered rabbit in smoked bacon with grilled veg.

20 Wishes for 2012

Design agency: Sophia Georgopoulou
Designer: Sophia Georgopoulou
Client: Personal work
Date: 2011
Location: Greece

20 wishes for 2012. 20 posters.1 calendar wrapped around wine bottles.
The wine-calendar bottles of 2012 were given as Christmas gifts to Sophia's
friends and clients in printed beige cotton pouches.
The illustrations and the visuals were taken (and were inspired by) Sophia's blog
"Sophia's Daily Thoughts" .

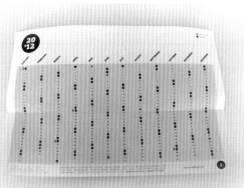

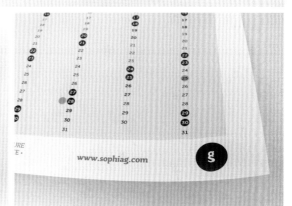

Design agency: Manic
Designer: Ji Jun, Wong Chee Yi, Jong Ling, Benjamin Koh, Winnie Dang,
           June Roland Baldavino, Roxanne Wee
Client: personal work
Date: 2011
Location: Singapore

This year, the designers put together a very limited run of these special Christmas kits for friends and clients at Manic. Each item is certified hand-made. This kit holds all of Manic's secret ingredients for a remarkable Christmas. Consumed correctly, this bundle will produce the most magical effects — eternal youth; a keen nose to guide you to the nearest bar; an outstanding sense of humour; and an insatiable desire to be merry. Seemed too good to be true? Take a look at the team, be dazzled by their spectacular charm and unending supply of good fortune. Effects are instant and last between six to twelve hours. Consume and take the night by storm, or kick-back and watch your stars align.

Ready to Fight!

Design agency: Great Advertising Group
Designer: Andrey Mordovtsev
Client: Onninen
Date: 2011
Location: Russia

This is a gift to customers and partners of Onninen company on the "Day of the Soviet Army and Navy" (February 23). In Russia it is traditionally considered as Men's day, similar to the March 8 - Women's Day. Inside original packing, shaped like AK-47 magazine, there are small bottles of vodka.

Northink Holiday Gift

Design agency: Northink
Designer: Catherine McLeod
Client: Catherine McLeod
Date: 2011
Location: Canada

This year for the Northink holiday gift the designer decided to celebrate the Canadian roots by giving clients Maple Syrup. The designer customized the bottles with labels that feature a vintage looking illustration of a Canadian landscape combined with Northink branding. The bottles were then placed in red tins and wrapped with a belly band made out of recycled paper.

Client Xmas Gift 2011 Wine Bottle

Design agency: BRND WGN
Designer: Karl Attard, Kris Vella Petroni
Client: personal work
Date: 2011
Location: Malta

What better way to celebrate a year ended than to put the highlights of
2011 in ink on paper and wrap it around very own hand-picked Private Estate
Selection, Cabernet Sauvignon from 2007. It's been a while since the client
worked on a publication so the designer really enjoyed working on this project
and printed two versions, one on standard news print paper and the other on
the same salmon hue paper used for the Financial Times. The top clients and
friends got a numbered bottle of which only 100 were produced whilst we also
sent a copy of BRND NWS (as we aptly called the newspaper to other contacts
of across the globe. It had some great feedback and would probably publish
BRND NWS again.

Louis XIII Rare Cask

Design agency: BETC Design
Designer: Sébastien Leridon
Client: Rémy Martin
Date: 2010
Location: France

The Louis XIII Rare Cask cognac by Rémy Martin is a gift box designed to encase the Louis XIII vintage of Rémy Martin cognac. The gift box is entirely dressed in a symbolic design that calls to mind the metal rings of a coat of mail. Its design is based on an innovative principle that draws on new technological processes and makes a radical break with the traditional practices of the world of fine spirits… by including two ramps of LEDs inside the casket to enhance and reveal the details of the decanter fashioned out of onyx (black Baccarat crystal). This gift box, limited edition of only 700 bottles, was crafted from noble materials (nickel-plated brass, fine leather with an embossed, hot silver-plated brand, a clasp forged from solid brass, a laser-etched polycarbonate mirror, black lacquered doors, etc).

Hudson Gavin Martin ©h®is™as

Design agency: Alt Group
Designer: Hudson Gavin Martin
Client: Onninen
Date: 2008
Location: New Zealand

Hudson Gavin Martin is a boutique legal practice formed by three partners, who advise on Intellectual Property and Technology Law. Culture and customs offer up all sorts of threesomes, humorous and otherwise. Core elements of the identity and tools of the intellectual property trade (the ©, ® and ™ symbols) were incorporated to spell Christmas. The concept of three is an important part of the brand. Christmas was stated three times and the gift itself was in three parts, wine, a rolling pin and a candle – all the ingredients for a celebration or three. A holy trinity if you will.

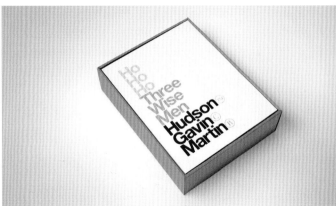

Art Director: Rob Ryan
Designer: Gemma Swift
Client: Wild & Wolf
Date: 2011
Location: UK

Licensed collection with Wild & Wolf.
Brand new two-colour screen printed mug.

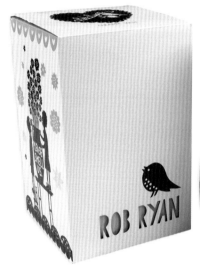

New Year Gift Set

Design agency: Artemov Artel graphic design bureau
Designer: Dasha Podoltseva
Client: Danfoss
Date: 2011
Location: Ukraine

This gift set used illustrative fairy tale stylistics, which makes joyful
festive mood.

Design agency: Artemov Artel Graphic Design Bureau
Designer: Oleksii Chernikov
Client: Danfoss
Date: 2011
Location: Ukraine

Corporate gift set consists of box of candies, paper bag and greeting card. Personal gift also includes branded vase. Spring floral ornaments were used to unite all elements of the gift set.

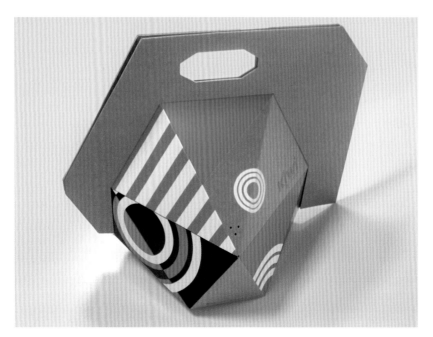

KIWI Packaging

Design agency: INCH KIEV
Art directors: Sergii Artemov, Gera Artemova
Designer: Rezo Gamrekelidze
Client: KIWI
Date: 2011
Location: Ukraine

KIWI produces very unusual and colourful gift talismans, therefore there was a need to develop packaging that matches its products and shows the company's individual approach to each piece. Besides that the package had to meet all technical requirements for transporting papier-mâché animals and be strong, big enough and even have special holes to let air in so their animals can breathe.

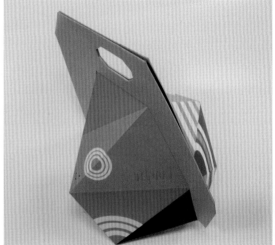

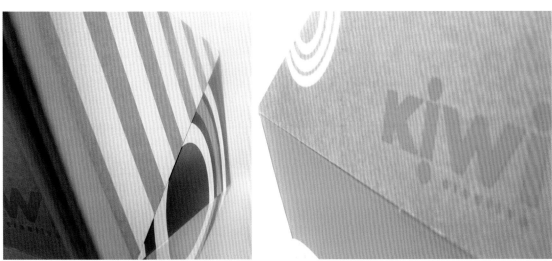

Cutting Edge

Design agency: Olle Sundin
Designer: Olle Sundin
Client: personal work
Date: 2010
Location: Sweden

A fictional flower shop oriented towards exclusive foreign flowers and plants with a scientific touch. The logo refers both to a flower and a molecular structure.

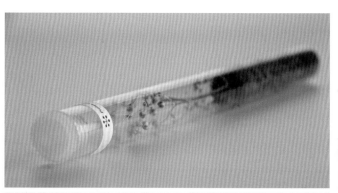

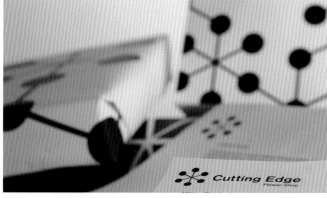

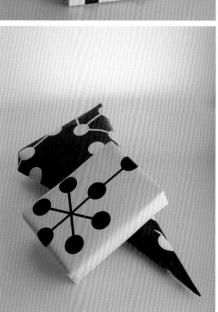

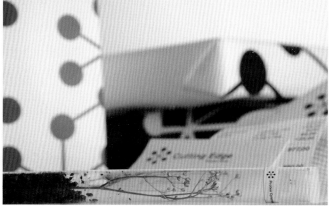

Design agency: Kaaita
Designer: Urska Hocevar
Client: Siemens Slovenia
Date: 2009
Location: Slovenia

Much of the additional waste headed to the landfill after the holiday season comes in the form of gift wrap and packaging. The alternative is not only to recycle, but to reuse. Siemens New Year Gift package is made of recycled paper and printed with water based inks. It is designed as 'a packet of inspiration' - as the sparks of creativity, encouraging the recipient to face the 'new', while also demonstrating the innovative nature of Siemens Corporation. Dot-It LED Light that comes with it transforms it into a portable lantern, that the gift recipient can use and enjoy long into the new year.

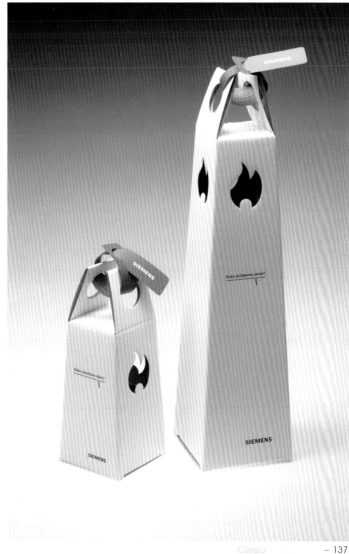

U&I Condoms

Designer: Yana Stepchenko
Client: U&I Condoms
Date: 2010
Location: Canada

The strategy revolves around the idea of making condoms really discrete and disguises them as though they were to appear to look like cosmetics product or even a jewelry case. By this way it removes the awkwardness and discomfort of purchasing condoms. The brand name "U&I" plays with the words communicating the closeness of two people. The package is compact and sustainable. It allows easy accessibility without having to take/shake out all the remaining condoms.

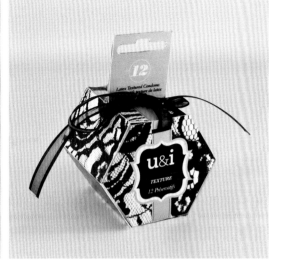

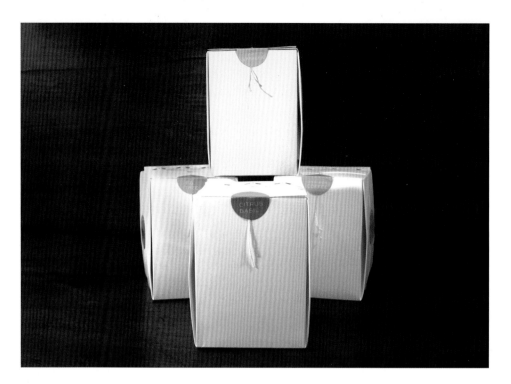

Sparrow Candles Packaging

Designer: Rachel Brinkman
Client: Sparrow Candles, San Antonio, Texas
Date: 2011
Location: Canada

This packaging system was designed to meet the needs of the owner of a small, specialty candle business. Since the business is owned and operated by one woman, the client expressed the need for a packaging system that would be inexpensive, appropriate to use as gift-packaging, and easily made in-house. The designer designed a packaging system that fits those needs by using a glueless, origami-inspired, custom box design that can be made from virtually any thick stock of paper. Due to the business's limited production and frequent scent changes, the packaging system is modular, easily modified to fit different candle sizes, and simple and natural in its aesthetic to echo the quality of the product.

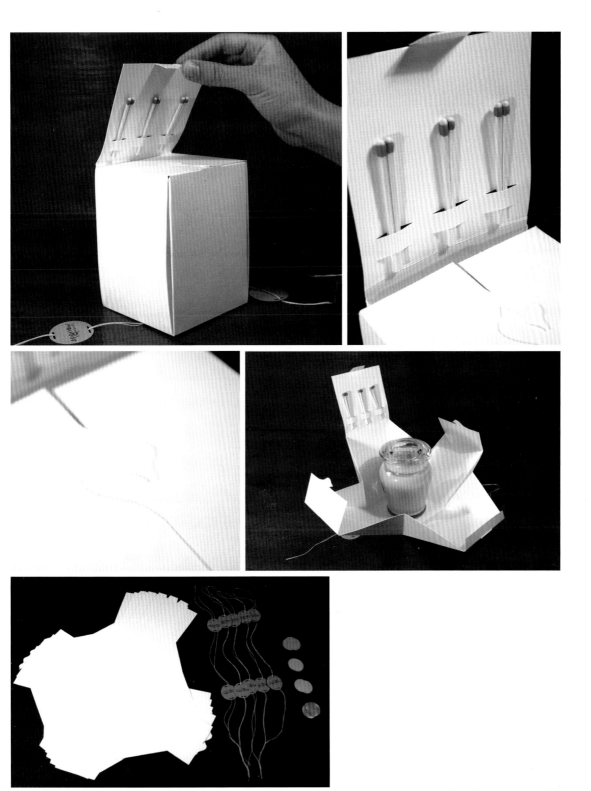

Candle Packaging

Design agency: KAA Design Group, Inc.
Designer: Annette Lee
Client: Tucker & Marks, Inc.
Date: 2008
Location: USA

It is a series of candle packaging design. The colour schemes of exterior and interior are highly contrast, yet are complement with each other. Only a hint of accent colour is revealed through the seam and created an interest. Ribbons are chosen to match the candle box interior colour.

Gift for Christmas 2008

Design agency: Zoo Studio
Designer: Xavier Castells
Client: Zoo Studio
Date: 2008
Location: Spain

It is a promotional gift for Christmas.

Design agency: HDI Youth Marketeers
Designer: Stephanie Mazingi
Client: HDI
Date: 2011
Location: South Africa

This is charitable and socially responsible client birthday gift. The idea is that whenever the client has a great idea they put money into the pig, and at the end of the year the company will go around collecting all the Paco's, match the money collected and donate it all to a specific children's home. This encourages great ideas from people and helps them contribute towards a good cause.

With Compliments for BFS

Design agency: Marin Santic
Designer: Marin Santic
Client: Brac Fini Sapuni
Date: 2009
Location: Croatia

Package is made from quality paper and folded without glue. It gives a
very original, unique and natural feeling. The paper tag can be printed on
demand and customised according to the customer's needs. The same
is with the rope that goes with it. It can also be in any colour, matching the
soap or the tag.

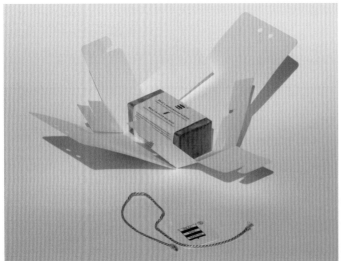

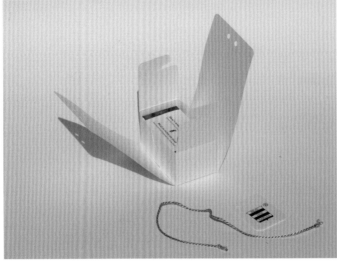

Transformer Box

Design agency: INCH KIEV
Designer: Anna Cherevko
Client: VESNA Workshop
Date: 2011
Location: Ukraine

This box can be used for lots of things; its six compartments can easily form a pyramid, as well as something more extravagant. The main benefit of this gift box construction is its functionality: since all its compartments can be opened separately, you can use it for storage as well. The agency presents it filled with objects of daily necessity. Guess what? Look at the design! Right! This is the box for women's panties.

Jeffrey Campbell Shoe Gift Box

Designer: Katy Verbrugge
Client: Personal work
Date: 2011
Location: USA

This gift box design was created for Jeffrey Campbell Shoes as a student project. Katy Verbrugge selected the Jeffrey Campbell brand because she loves the unique, creative, bold colours, styles and design. The brand is all about a tremendous love for shoes by those with a creative sense of style. Katy Verbrugge wanted to show off their unique, artistic style by creating watercolour and hand-drawn illustrations. This is a box that would be in a boutique for when you want to give (or receive) Jeffrey Campbell shoes as a gift! Katy Verbrugge designed it this way because shoes are a gift that you buy yourself and it should feel like opening a present. Katy Verbrugge also added a scratch-off element under the lid to provide an interactive experience. When you scratch it off, it reveals a fun quote about shoes. Katy Verbrugge utilised the Jeffrey Campbell signature in combination with the illustration work to create a bright, memorable, and iconic box design.

Shoe love is true love

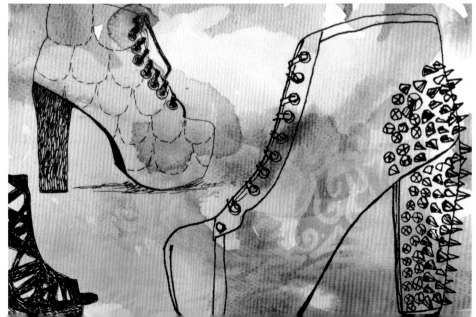

Gift Box

Design agency: Ark Ceramic Art Ltd
Designer: Gordon Mckenna
Client: personal work.
Date: 2011
Location: UK

These gift boxes are bespoke made from sturdy black card and have the company logo Ark Ceramic Art Ltd. in silver on the lid. The boxes work great with the smaller items and turn a simple gift into something far more special. It also means that the customers can send a gift directly from the Etsy shop. The designer have had box sizes made up that work well with all kinds of gift: buttons, Christmas ornaments and pendants (pendant necklaces with silver findings and bales already include a gift box).

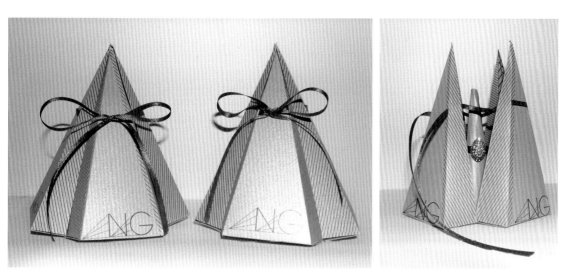

Nue Gallery Jewellery

Design agency: Kristy Jean Design
Designer: Kristy Birtwistle
Client: Nue Gallery
Date: 2011
Location: Australia

The brief was to create a brand for concept a jewellery company, Nue Galley, and to then use this as inspiration for packaging to suit a range of rings. The client wanted to express exclusivity and high quality within the jewellery industry, so the brand had to be modern, sleek and elegant.

The original brand concept came from the idea of light refracting off of a diamond, which also gave the package its shape and unique opening mechanism. This idea of light changing direction was also a great metaphor for the packages' subject, an engagement ring, as the intention to marry is often a new direction or chapter in one's life.

Jersey Pearl Jewellery Packaging

Design agency: Morgan Agency
Designer: David Coupland
Client: Jersey Pearl
Date: 2010
Location: UK

Jersey Pearl has been established as a pearl showroom for 25 years and took the decision to grow its business through selling its own collections of jewellery into independent retailers throughout the UK. In order to achieve this David Coupland designed and art directed sales brochures, direct mail and packaging.

ZARA Gift Card & Packing

Design agency: thisismaurix
Designer: Carlos Mauricio Domínguez
Client: Inditex Group • Zara
Date: 2011
Location: Spain

The whole renewal of the image of Zara, including the website & stores, also needed a gift card redesign, according to the new image. This concept aims to connect with the costumer by being more actual & fresh. A calligraphic logotype mixed with classic Zara elements, including little details such as the silk paper, special inks & a luxury bag, make this gift card, a real present itself. The designer also created a DT4 iron display, with a special treatment to achieve a used look, to show the gift card in the stores, including a silver silkscreened card in different languages for each country.

Jewelery Gift

Design agency: JULIANA DUQUE DISEÑO
Designer: Juliana Duque Gennrich
Client: ORGE A. LIÉVANO JOYERÍAi
Date: 2011
Location: Colombia

A jewel is not just a gift, it's a whole experience. The designer wanted the package to be representative of the quality of the gift it was carrying, something expensive and unique, but also wanted to keep low production costs. First, the suede cases were monogramed inside. The designer created two types of gift boxes: square (for ring, earrings and necklaces), and long for bracelets. Each box comes in both grey and gold. The suede boxes are placed in a bed of silk paper (printed with gold monograms) and the box is closed with a turquoise satin sash. The final touches include a monogram tag (that doubles as a gift card on the back) and a gold sticker on a turquoise shopping bag. The bag is also filled with the monogramed silk paper for a gift that feels both elegant and special.

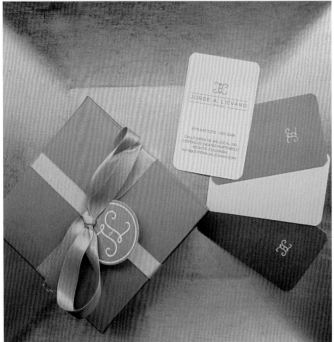

Design agency: Binder Gestão Estratégica
Designer: Marcos Behrens
Client: Leite de Rosas
Date: 2009
Location: Brazil

When a company celebrates 80 years of life, it has only one thing to say: thank you.
Leite de Rosas is a traditional Brazilian cosmetics brand and in 2009 celebrated its 80 years. To honour its tradition and the family company feeling that the brand has until today, they organized a mass to celebrate this date. This was a very private event, only to the family of the founders, partners, clients and opinion leaders. The client´s request for the occasion was a formal and elegant, wedding like invitation, and along with it a rosary would be given as a gift.

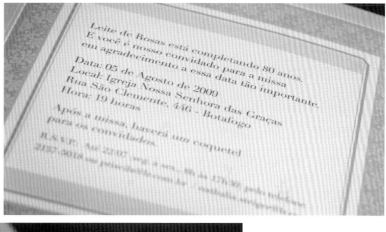

Leite de Rosas está completando 80 anos.
E você é nosso convidado para a missa
em agradecimento a essa data tão importante.

Data: 05 de Agosto de 2009
Local: Igreja Nossa Senhora das Graças
Rua São Clemente, 446 - Botafogo
Hora: 19 horas

Após a missa, haverá um coquetel
para os convidados.

R.S.V.P.: Até 22/07, seg. a sex., 9h às 17h30, pelo telefone
2152-9018 ou pmedvedovsky.com.br · recibida obrigatória

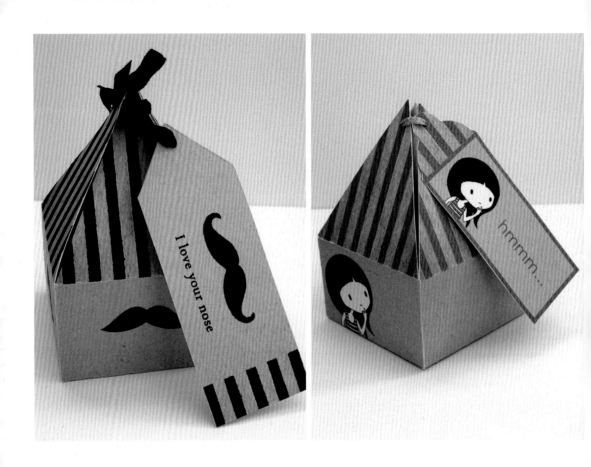

Small Gift Boxes For Jewellery

Design agency: The Inklings of Tess
Designer: Tessa Farlow
Client: The Inklings of Tess
Date: 2011
Location: UK

The designer is the owner of a small business called 'The Inklings of Tess'. She is an illustrator and also sell jewellery with the images on. As well as being an illustrator, she is also passionate about packaging. These boxes were originally designed as gift wrap for her jewellery products but they were so successful on Etsy that now she sell them separately.

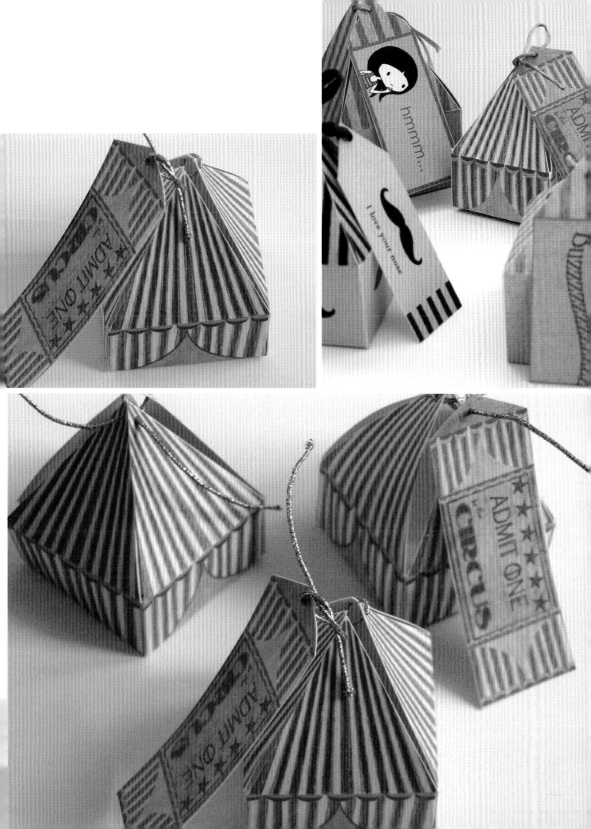

Family Christmas Gift 2010

Design agency: Family Design Co.
Designer: Trent Sunderland, Michelle Harper, Ellie Hemmings
Client: Family Design Co.
Date: 2011
Location: New Zealand

Being the first Christmas gift as Family Design Co., the designer wanted to reinforce the message behind Family Design Co.'s new brand and give clients something they would be proud to wear. The idea 'Family Ties' was born as the designer believe that is what brings us all together at Christmas time. Creating four different designs for ladies and men, alternating them between black and white t-shirts, packaged in a black or white box with die-cut window to reveal only the tie design. Wrap-around label introducing 'Family Ties' along with ribbon and card attached to each shirt.

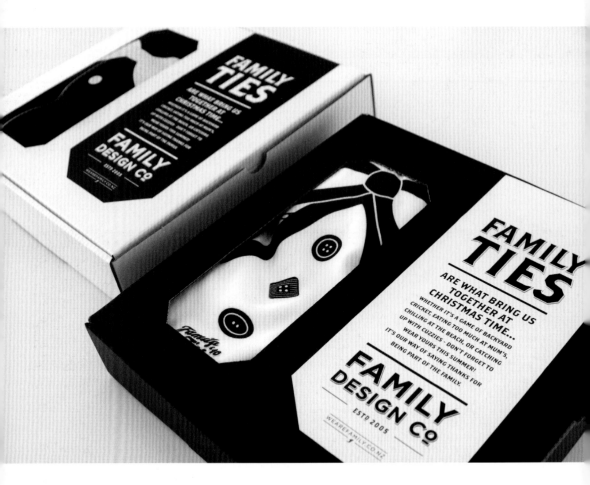

WISHING YOU AND YOUR FAMILY A WONDERFUL CHRISTERFUL CHRISTMAS & PROSPEROUS & NEW YEAR

Family Ties

New York Subway

Design agency: Shiho Masuda Style and Design
Designer: Shiho Masuda
Client: private collection
Date: 2011
Location: Japan

The package was created based on a request from an individual client for gift wrapping her souvenirs in a New York City theme. The map and subway card were used during a client's trip to the city and she wanted to include them as a part of her gift. Coloured paper twine mirrors the subway lines on the map as they playfully tie around the box.

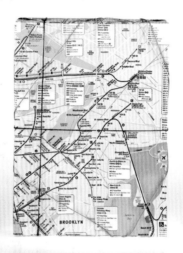

GraphicSpeaks New Year Scarf Gift Box

Design agency: To Be Designed Co., Ltd
Designer: Natthawit Tongprasert
Client: GraphicSpeaks
Date: 2011
Location: Thailand

New Year gift especially designed for GraphicSpeaks consisted of limited edition scarf which was designed to make income donating to flood victims in Thailand via Thai Red Cross.

The Santa Claus *(Christmas Gift for Sid Lee's clients)*

Design agency: Sid Lee
Designer: Philippe Dubuc
Client: Sid Lee
Date: 2010
Location: Canada

For Christmas 2010, renowned Quebec fashion king Philippe Dubuc designed a scarf exclusively for the agency's clients. The Santa Claus packaging meets the following two objectives: express Christmas cheer and accentuate the scarf itself, keeping it light on the packaging. The concept focuses on the scarf's design and, more specifically, on the zipper, which doubles as Santa's mouth. Also, the fact that the dentures aren't attached to the rest of the packaging adds to the fun of unwrapping the gift. Finally, a greeting card accompanied the gift and illustrated three fun ways to wear the scarf.

Women'secret Press Gift

Design agency: Base Design
Designer: Friedel Scholten
Client: Women'secret
Date: 2011
Location: Spain

Client Women'secret is a fashion brand specializing in underwear, swimwear, and lingerie. Collection of press gifts designed and produced for Women'secret. Each season Women'secret announces the new collections to the press. Base has conceptualised, designed and produced objects that are a wink of the collection and are linked to the season. The object contains a garment in its interior.

Tout Sweet Boutique

Design agency: The Savannah College of Art and Design
Designer: Becca Millern
Client: Personal work
Date: 2011
Location: USA

The Tout Sweet Boutique is a mock company that produces high quality, design accessories for little girls between the ages of five and twelve. The intention behind the product is to celebrate a girly, fantastical youth that is desired for little girls. Each product is intended to endure childhood and last a lifetime. As a child, receiving a gift is always elating but sometimes the package of gift comes in can be equally as memorable. The designer designed each package to function as an antique hatbox. In order to reveal the treasure inside, the lucky little princess who received the gift has to untie the silk bow and relieve the lid from the box. Each boxes interior is lined with silk. The silk lining highlights the preciousness of the present and encourages the boxes to be kept.

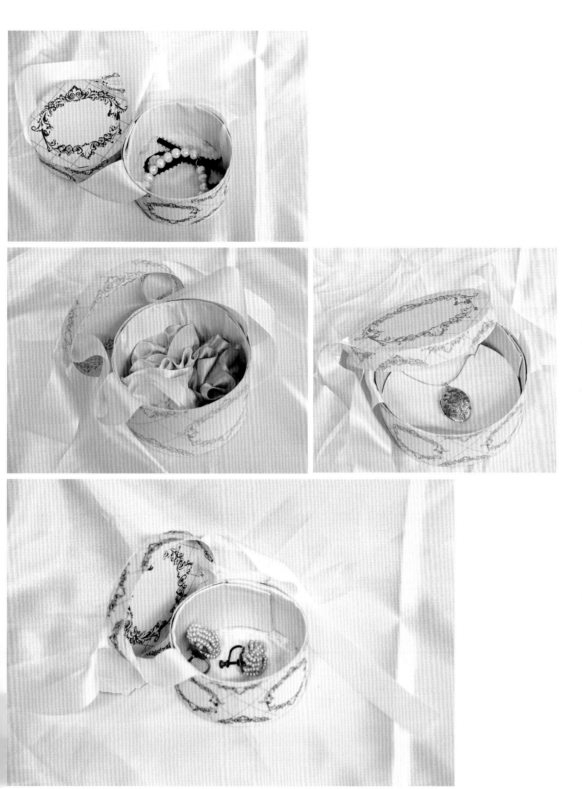

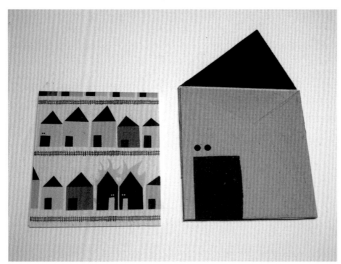

Getting on Like a House on Fire

Design agency: Emily Darby
Designer: Emily Darby
Client: personal work
Date: 2011
Location: UK

This personal brief was to design an aesthetically pleasing stationery range using commonly known phrases as the theme, giving them a fun twist and without making the messages too obvious. The phrase that chose for the wrapping paper was 'getting on like a house on fire'. The designs have some hand drawn elements but are mainly made from cutting and sticking coloured card and scanning them.

CD Packaging Gift Set

Design agency: Studio Baklazan
Designer: urszula kluz-knopek
Client: Personal work
Date: 2011
Location: Poland

The graphic was printed on a metal box. It was specially made to adorn a CD with barroque music, and the structure is compared to a pearl with irregular shape. The masterpieces that were recorded on the CD are compositions of French and German artists. Despite they all belong to the same epoque a listener can hear subtle differences in style. The recording is an invitation to a journey through France and Germany of the 18th century, which contains the essence of European barroque music.

Matter 2012 New Year Package

Design agency: Matter Strategic Design
Designer: Mike Kasperski
Client: Matter Strategic Design
Date: 2011
Location: Canada

One of the most interesting things about Matter Strategic Design's 2011/2012 holiday gift is the fact that it's not a holiday gift at all. It's a cleverly packaged collection of 'ideas journals' in celebration of the New Year. And, as with the firm's past seasonal gifts, arrived in clients' mailboxes well after the mayhem of the holiday period had worn off. The package is a zipper-perforated mailer that separates the year '12' into parts '1' and '2'. Once opened, the mailer reveals two beautiful notebooks and a personalised letter encouraging the recipient to keep one and share the other with someone who matters to them.

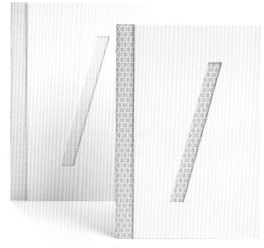

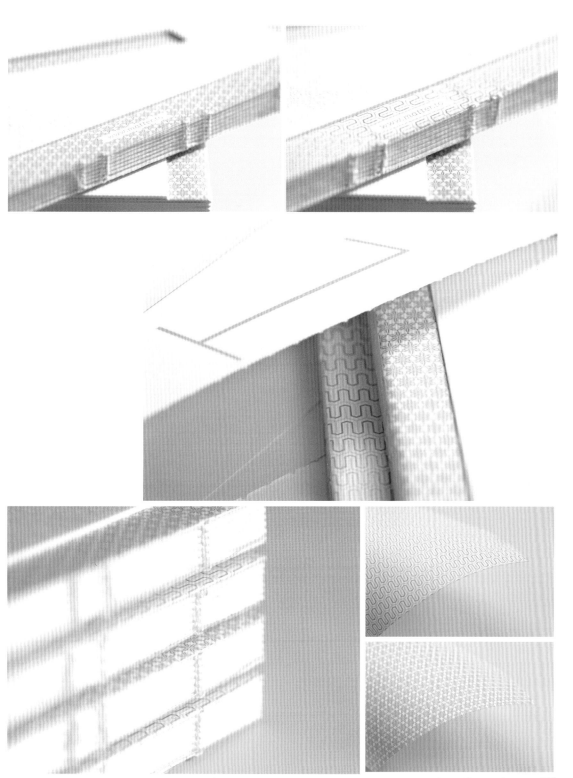

Corbis Christmas Pack

Design agency: Inhouse
Designer: Katrin Bohlinger
Client: Corbis
Date: 2009
Location: UK

A gift for loyal clients, this box set included a card set and wrapping paper that featured exclusive imagery from corbis.com. The gift box was localised in UK, France, Germany, Italy, The Netherlands, Poland.

Valentine's Day Box

Design agency: Tiana Avila Design
Designer: Tiana Avila
Client: personal work
Date: 2010
Location: USA

The concept of this project was to make an item and/or package that relates to Valentine's Day. The designer created a sentimental Valentine to be given away. Inside the main Valentine's Day box is three smaller boxes that are meant to be given away to someone you love. The giveaway boxes are complete with a booklet and dried flowers that the person receiving the box can plant in their garden. The dried flowers have seeds inside that symbolize encouraged growth and something to look forward to in the future. Giving flower seeds is a simple gesture to symbolise the future that you want to have with your loved one. With the hand stitching and homemade quality of the packaging, it gives a special, personalised feeling to whomever you give it to.

Open Easy! A New Year Gift to Customers and Partners

Design agency: Great Advertising Group
Designer: Andrey Mordovtsev
Client: Aeroc
Date: 2008
Location: Russia

The original package contains a calendar, caviar and opener for cans. The bright colour packaging and calendar in harmony with the colour of caviar, and gives warmth in cold winter.

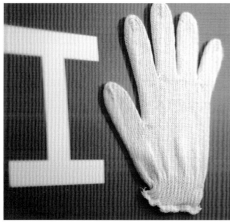

O2 Broadband Promotional Pack

Design agency: RR Donnelley Ireland
Designer: Alan Conlan, Feena McCarthy
Client: O2 Ireland
Date: 2011
Location: Ireland

O2 came to RR Donnelley with a great challenge – to try to explain to Carphone Warehouse staff why they should be selling O2 broadband and not a competitor's broadband. The designer thought it would be nice to give them a gift, as well as presenting all the reasons they should be selling O2 broadband in a clear concise booklet. The designer wrapped up the booklet and a 1GB usb wristband in a sleek silver box. A premium, easy to understand pack which could essentially be used as a reference tool when needed. The designer made the pack and information more memorable with a gift of a wristband USB key for the staff member. Working within strict O2 brand guidelines, the designer pushed the boundaries to make the pack premium, memorable and unusual. The piece was designed to be something that the staff would like to keep and reuse.

Aztec Gift Wrap Set

Design agency: WitShop
Designer: Jakob Creswell-Rost, Freya Hawtin
Client: personal work
Date: 2011
Location: UK

This colourful wrapping set consists of a quality sheet of wrapping paper with contrasting Aztec style printed card. The set also comes complete with recycled gift tag, envelope and natural raffia ribbon. That will make any gift look and feel extra bit special.

Advertising Field - 7 Years

Design agency: Dmitry Syzonenko, Pavel Petel
Designer: Dmitry Syzonenko, Pavel Petel
Client: Media Holding
Date: 2007
Location: Ukraine

The company has been established for seven years, and needed an original gift for clients. The designer decided to create the design of the seven CD packages. Each envelope is one year. To get the music CD you want to open all seven packages. The company and its customers were very satisfied.

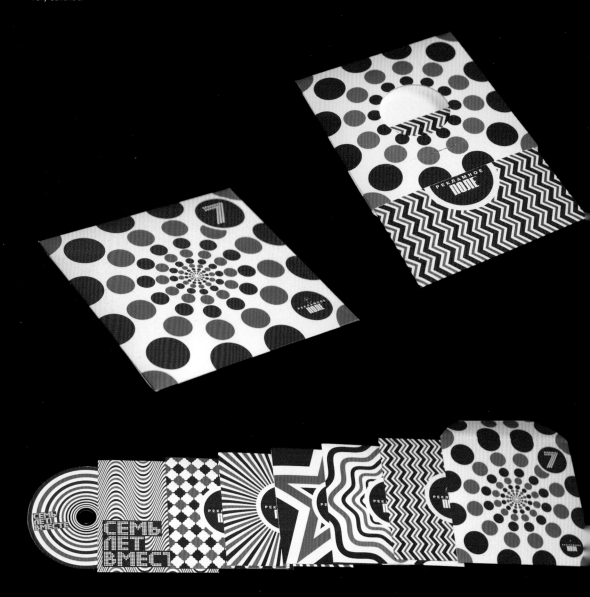

Groovewear Artist Box

Design agency: LA TIGRE
Designer: Walter Molteni
Client: Groovewear
Date: 2010
Location: Italy

Groovewear special edition box contains a limited edition tee shirt and silkscreen by famous European street artists. Each issue includes fine papers, special printing techniques and custom numbers.

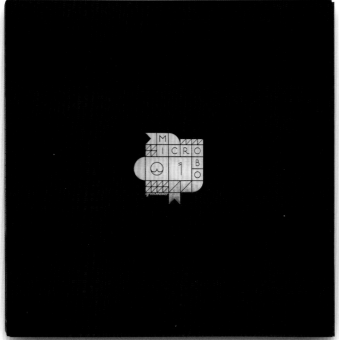

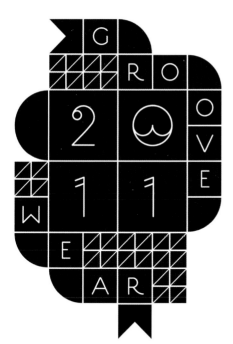

Design agency: Areaveinte
Designer: Yanina V. Arias
Client: personal work
Date: 2011
Location: Argentina

To celebrate the holidays of 2011, the designers wanted to give their customers a special present but also very useful in working hours. Moreover, the idea was that everything was produced by the designers themselves.
The designers thought and launched their creativity... so they decided to develop a notebook, in this way the customers could write the best ideas everyday!
These notebooks were produced entirely by hand, one by one. The designers bought textured paper (black and orange), did the silkscreen´s printing and then they banded all of it.
In addition, the designers wanted to have a special wrap, crepe paper and ribbons to give a nice texture to the touch. Obviously with the beautiful colours that identify the designers themselves!
They had so much fun ... hope you like it!
Here some photos...

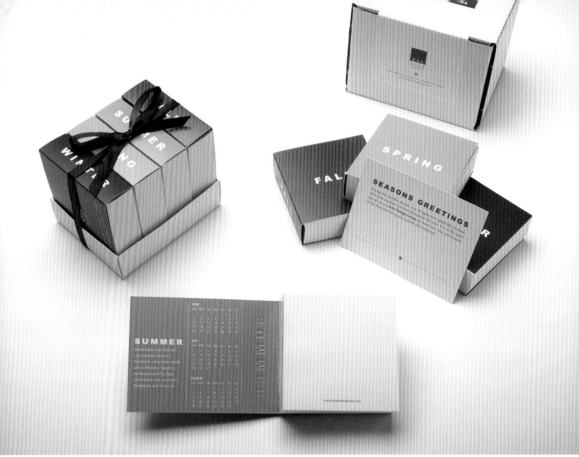

Seasonal Calendar

Design agency: KAA Design Group, Inc.
Designer: Annette Lee, Louis-Philippe Carretta
Client: KAA Design Group, Inc.
Date: 2006
Location: USA

Seasonal calendars are packaged in a customised tray with year embossed.

Best Gift Ever

Design agency: Marina Androsovich
Designer: Marina Androsovich
Client: Best Gift Ever
Date: 2011
Location: Russia

The company 'Best Gift Ever' suggests adventures as gifts. So, the main points to focus on were adventure, experience, wonder. How could these issues be reflected in such thing as packaging? In order to cause some associations with emotional sphere, several abstract shapes were created. Differentiation is achieved through diversity of forms and has logical connections with relevant sphere. For sport activities, for example, more dynamic shape was developed, whereas beauty direction was supported with flowing lines. The colour of texture is direction specific: the beauty line demands more natural, wood-like tones, informative activities - energetic red, and icy blue for extreme activities.

Gift Kit Address Book Grpcom 2012

Design agency: The Getz
Designer: Raphael Rodrigues da Silva
Client: Grpcom
Date: 2011
Location: Brazil

Every year the communication group Grpcom gives to its customers an exclusive diary as gift. For 2012 the diary theme was Attitude Every Day, suggesting that each day you can make all things better with positive attitudes. A calendar also was given in the kit box.

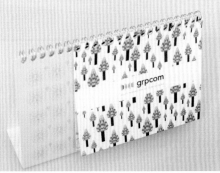

Christmas Snowball Fight

Design agency: Barker Gray
Designer: Tom Collins
Client: Barker Gray
Date: 2010
Location: Australia

The 'Office Snowball Fight' concept offered to bring some of the fun of a traditional northern hemisphere winter to the clients in the Southern hemisphere, baking in the heat of the summer. The 'snowballs' were made up of waste paper from studio. When unwrapped they revealed some of the unsuccessful ideas that didn't quite make the cut – amongst other delicious treats. The packaging was inspired by the English Victorian period and the charming imagery and language from that time. In keeping with the era, the tub was gift-wrapped in simple brown paper and string before being delivered in bundles.

Wood Gift Wrap Set

Design agency: WitShop
Designer: Jakob Creswell-Rost, Freya Hawtin
Client: personal work
Date: 2010
Location: UK

This natural looking wrapping set comes with a sheet of brown kraft wood grain printed paper and a striking hand drawn blank greeting card. The set also contains a recycled envelope, gift tag and natural raffia ribbon in complimentary purple hues.

Future Champion-baptism Invitation and More

Design agency: Sophia Georgopoulou
Designer: Sophia Georgopoulou
Client: Ilias Sarantos, Marina Giareni
Date: 2011
Location: Greece

The baby-girl invited all people to attend her first tournament and she introduces herself as a future champion of tennis. The concept of this invitation derived from the her father's occupation (tennis instructor) as well as the godfather's hobby! A big cockade pin was used on the invitation containing all the information of the baptism. Smaller cockade pins decorated the baptism giveaway gifts, the candles, the wish book and much more.

Zara Kiddy´s Class Gift Card

Design agency: Bandagesloveblood
Designer: Mar Martitegui
Client: Inditex Group • Zara
Date: 2011
Location: Spain

Zara Kids is now an important part of most of Zara stores all around the world, growing larger everyday. But there are still some stores just for Zara kids clothes under the name of Kiddy´s Class. These independent stores needed their own gift card. Taken in consideration the young client who will receive this card as a present the designer thought it had to be a cool design to attract the kid's attention. But it must maintain the elegant look, which characterizes Zara. And a simple packaging design to use in all the different applications. That´s why the designer used black & white on recycle paper & illustrated characters to connect with the kids. The gift envelope is a pyramidal design in recycled paper, printed inside with a 'monster' pattern to form part of the gift surprise. Inside the designer placed the gift card and the leaflet. The package is closed with a round sticker with one of the characters and the brand.

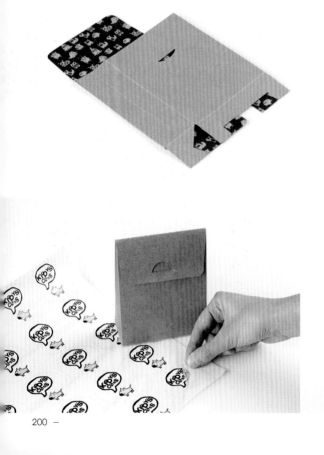

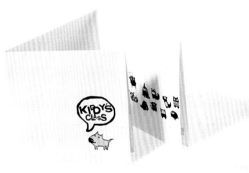

Tikou Tikou

Design agency: Aeraki
Designer: Despina Aeraki
Client: Patrick Malone, Antzela Galazoula
Date: 2007
Location: Greece

During the meeting with her mom and dad, the designer tried to discover the most cute details of little Katarina's personality. The designer picked up "tikou-tikou", out of her babytalk, to illustrate the invitation. the designer also drew a bear on it, as a bear-doll was her favorite toy. The fabric bib-invitations were offered as wrapped presents to the guests.

Kids Rule

Design agency: Five Talents Ltd
Designer: Lorelei Ragan
Client: Hallmark
Date: 2009
Location: UK

This small range of greeting cards and gift wrap were designed specifically for a personal project of the designer's whilst freelancing. Design of a range of cards for teenagers to encourage them to purchase cards for their friends rather than their parents to purchase them on their behalf. The range includes colourful, fun and cool imagery that will attract the demographic to send to their peers. The collection was small but the designer could see the potential of the range and it's possibilities. By using the baseball boot route gives the range a retro but hip feel to the design.

Together

Design agency: Aeraki
Designer: Despina Aeraki
Client: Georgos Aerakis, Vasia Athanasiou
Date: 2011
Location: Greece

Giorgos and Vassia were about to get married and christen both of their children, Angelos and Despina, at the same time. Designing a common invitation for the three ceremonies was a major creative challenge. The fact that the family had been already sharing love and strong bond between them for quite some time was the designer's main creational concept. A candle was the key object of the invitation, considering its flame as the flame of love. The precut family figures were to be attached at the notches around the candle and its light was supposed to pass through the heart-shaped windows of each figure. The invitation box also contained an instruction manual for putting the pieces together properly, as well as a red heart-shaped sticker for the guests' wishes. The favor was a paper-cut baby cube with the first four letters of the Greek alphabet, which also happen to be the name initials of the family members and the gift was a red heart with the family figures, made of plexiglass. Special paper horns were printed for the wedding ceremony and paper hearts were mixed into their rice filling; a special frame also created, allowing the guests to stick the invitation hearts with their wishes on it. The project was developed as an interactive game, starting the moment that the guest would open the invitation box and ending when he would stick his own wishes heart on the wishes frame.

Ας πάει η καρδιά στη θέση της...

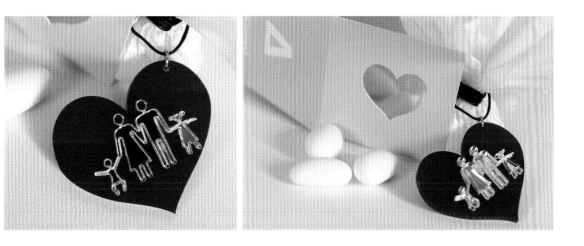

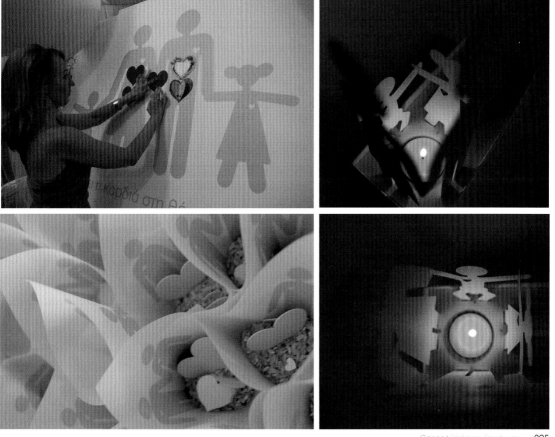

UNICEF Wrapping

Design agency: Diego-caio
Designer: Diego Oliveira
Client: UNICEF
Date: 2011
Location: Brazil & Italy

UNICEF wanted to increase donations by selling Inspired Gifts throughout the year and not just at Christmas. Inspired Gifts are life-saving items that UNICEF provides around the world. The UNICEF Wrapping Project was born out of the insight that people buy wrapping paper every time they buy a present. So when someone buys UNICEF wrapping paper they would actually be giving another gift. A real donation that supports the protection of children's rights. The wrapping papers also work as an alternative form of print advertising that require no media spend and promote the cause every time a present is received.

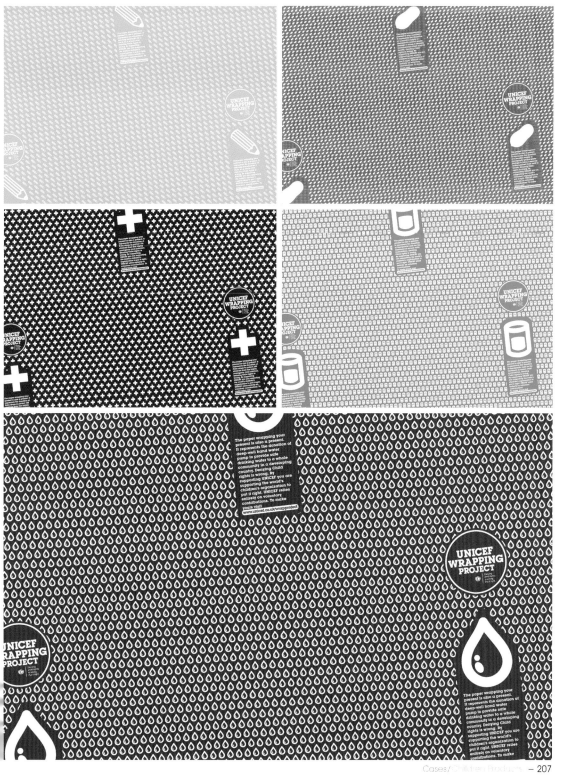

Design agency: MOZAIQ Eco Design
Designer: Janina Böhm
Client: personal work
Date: 2011
Location: Germany

As a designer, you can actively pursue environmental protection by creating products which are made from environmentally friendly materials. And especially when it comes to paper goods such as wrapping paper, which has a very short lifetime, it is an important aspect to think about. That's why the design studio MOZAIQ creates and distributes ecofriendly paper goods of a high quality and timeless design. These wrapping papers and gift tags are printed with vegetable-based inks on 100% recycled paper.

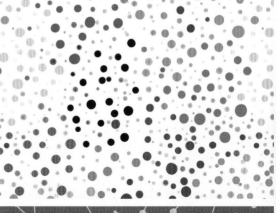

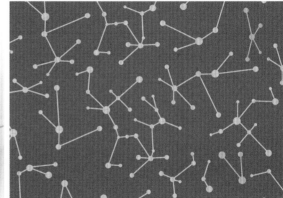

Candy Time

Designer: Amnon Owed
Client: personal work
Date: 2011
Location: The Netherlands

Candy Time is a cheerful and delicious gift packaging design that conveys joy to the viewer. The atmosphere of celebration that surrounds precious gifts is further enhanced by the chosen theme. A limited yet striking colour palette is selected to strengthen the feeling of happiness. The idea for this pattern came about through a free association mindmap. It only takes a few simple steps to freely associate from wrapping paper to presents, then to party and finally to candy! Seemingly obvious in retrospect, it just makes perfect sense. And more importantly, it provides a beautiful and festive gift packaging design for all to enjoy.

Design agency: Dez Propaganda
Designer: Camila Andrade Scroferneker
Client: Farmácia Angeloni
Date: 2010
Location: Brazil

Every year the Brazilian pharmacy chain Angeloni develops special
packaging for the summer. In 2010, the client assigned the agency
with a challenging task: create something inspired by the sunny season
to ornate the regular craft bags they already had. As well as that,
the designs should be easily identifiable as women's and men's. Dez
Propaganda came up with caps that could be stapled over the bag
after the products had been placed inside it. In both male and female
lines the designer used lively and colourful graphics that related to the
season: tones of pink, reds and flowery shapes for women; blues and sea
elements for men. In the end, it worked so well.

Design agency: ANDREYKOVAL
Designer: Andrey Koval
Client: Lilac
Date: 2010
Location: Ukraine

Gift bags for the project Lilac. The unique design and illustration. Used cardboard, scissors, rapidograph, thread, cringle, and gouache. Size: 21cmx14cmx7cm.

Candy Stripe

Design agency: Studio Kudos
Designer: Studio Kudos
Client: personal work
Date: 2010
Location: USA

Studio Kudos designed a typographic wrapping paper, a holiday series. Large striped graphics numbers eight and nine, rendered in fluorescent pink and metallic gold. Candy Stripe is part of holiday gifting tradition started in 2008.

Party Faces/ Festival Wrapping Paper

Design agency: ANDREYKOVAL.com
Designer: Bel's Art World
Client: personal work
Date: 2011
Location: UK

This wrapping paper is based on designer's small self-produced zine 'Faces' with the theme of exploring different faces from music festivals and parties around the world. A celebration of lively, colourful characters on light brown sugar paper. Hand silk-screen printed in dark pink & turquoise.

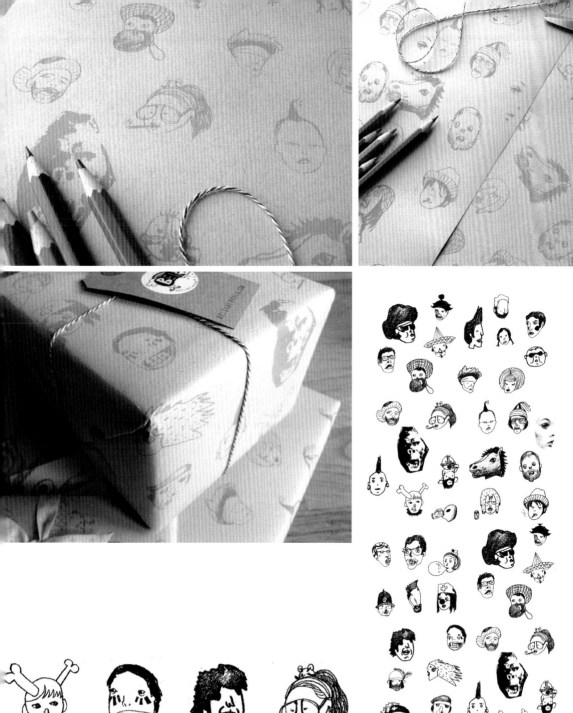

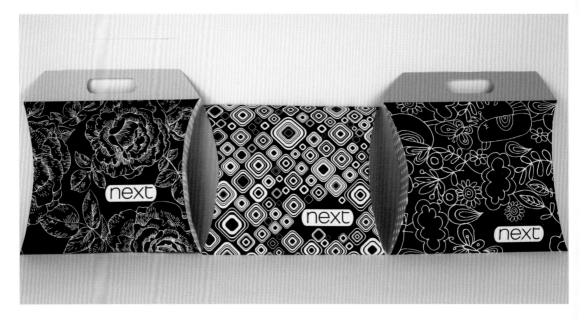

Gift Bag for "NEXT"

Designer: Dessi Keane
Client: personal work
Date: 2010
Location: UK

The gift bags are designed for Next, a British department store. Meant for their summer season they are different for male, female and children's products.

Italian Greyhound Holiday Set

Design agency: Karyn Jimenez-Elliott Design
Designer: Karyn Jimenez-Elliott
Client: East Coast Italian Greyhound Rescue
Date: 2011
Location: USA

All of the illustrations are hand done with micron pen on vellum, and it is printed on Neenah Environment Paper, Desert Storm. All proceeds from the sales went to the East Coast Italian Greyhound Rescue.

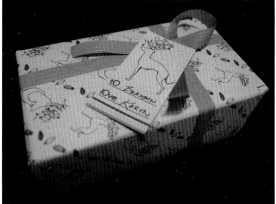

Design agency: ZWEIZUEINS / molter&sartor
Designer: Marika Molter, Ina Sartor, Andreas Magino, Katharina Sussek
Client: personal work
Date: 2008
Location: Germany

This is a collection of three different wrapping papers. The design interprets the subject of giving and receiving in a typographic and illustrative manner and moreover makes sure that unwrapping the gift is a pleasant surprise. According to the requirements the wrapping paper can be used from both sides and thereby allows a slightly different perspective on the tradition of making a gift.

Gift Wrap

Design agency: Full Drop Collective
Designer: Elise Cakebread, Sophie Curtain, Megan McNeill, Ella Schwartz, LaniSommer, and Yolanda Zarins
Client: personal work
Date: 2011
Location: Australia

This project was designed and printed by the Full Drop Collective to raise money for their graduate show. The individual and unique collection of gift wrap was hand screen printed using left over print paste from their university print room. It comes as a mixed pack of four sheets, each measuring 594mm x 841mm.

Giftwrap Paper Leafs & Flowers

Designer: Kim Welling
Client: Kim's Little Monsters
Date: 2011
Location: The Netherlands

Giftwrap paper for webshop with leafs and flowers design; giftwrap paper
with divers antler designs; giftwrap paper with pigs flying through the
clouds; giftwrap paper with different faces.

Designer: Luisa Arango
Client: Amor Amor
Date: 2011
Location: Colombia

These gift wrapping papers are part of Amor Amor collection, which specialises in illustrative products.

The monster designs started with a hand drawn sketch which was scanned and then edited in illustrator. Once finished was hand screen printed with water based inks on 60 gsm recycled brown kraft paper for the polychrome designs and white paper for the monochrome designs.

The white paper was designed with a purpose of self drawing, so the user can create a unique final piece.

Break Up Cards

Designer: Michelle Gray
Client: personal work
Date: 2011
Location: USA

The designer created a set of cards to send to someone when you want to break up with them as well as wrapping paper to use when you send back their unwanted gifts. The Break Up Card set was designed to look happy on the outside until opened, that is when you realise it is not the happy scenario you were picturing.

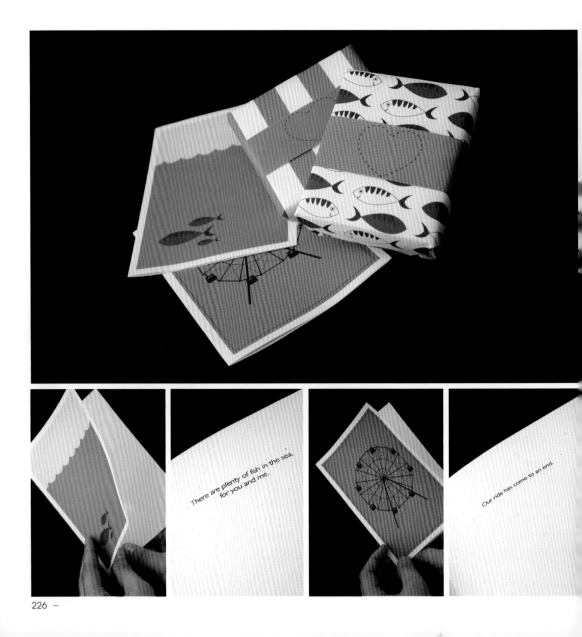

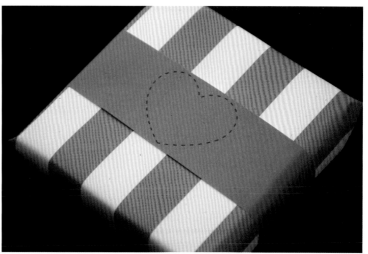

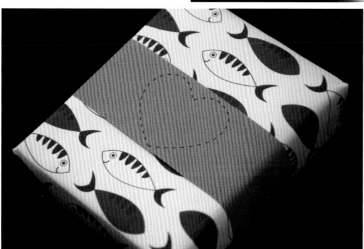

Maxway Promotional Gift Set

Design agency: Artemov Artel Graphic Design Bureau
Art directors: Sergii Artemov, Gera Artemova
Designer: Oleksii Chernikov
Client: Maxway Production Company
Date: 2008
Location: Ukraine

Maxway Production Company provides high complexity polygraphic works (foil stamping, multilevel stamping, pattern printing etc.). Special promotional gift set was designed to demonstrate company's services during REX 2008 international exhibition. Gift set consists of paper bag, 'Flower' promotional gift, 'Butterfly' business card, decorative box for 'Flower' gift and 'Butterfly' card.

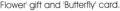

2012 New Year Wrapping Paper

Design agency: Mediacrat
Designer: Elena Bulay
Client: Mediacrat
Date: 2011
Location: Russia

Russian ad agency 'Mediacrat' is greeting its friends, clients and partners on 2012 New Year with bottles of wine wrapped in this kraft paper. Everyone makes a personal greeting. Elena Bulay drew a pattern (Christmas decorations, spruce branches, greetings) and a dragon in the center of paper.

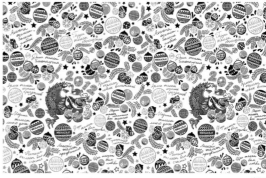

Martian Wrapping Paper

Design agency: SicolaMartin
Designer: Oen Hammonds, Felipe Villela
Client: SicolaMartin
Date: 2010
Location: USA

SicolaMartin wanted to create a holiday gift that reflected the agency personality and respected a variety of traditions – so SicolaMartin created cool giftwrap for any celebration, from Christmas to Kwanzaa. The designs derived from the SicolaMartin brand identity that of 'Martians,' a play the agency's name.

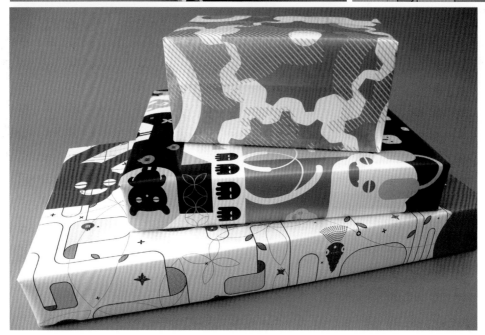

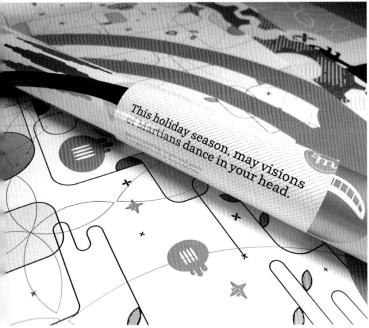

This holiday season, may visions of Martians dance in your head.

'Card Pocket' Gift Bag Collection

Design agency: American Greetings Corporation
Designer: Esther Loopstra
Client: American Greetings Corporation
Date: 2010
Location:USA

This was a gift bag collection sold in various grocery stores and convenience stores. The bags were created to be able to hold a normal size greeting card on the front of the bag. Concepting, surface design and illustrations, product development and design were done by Esther Loopstra.

Festival Gift Bags

Design agency: Petek Design
Designer: Efrat Elie
Client: Petek Design
Date: 2010
Location: Israel

A revolutionary idea that had a great success - prefect & cute gift bag for various kinds of festivals. Ideal for small gifts such as candies, cookies, jewelry or any other fun gesture for your loved ones. It can be PDF file, sent to each customer via email, and self printed on A4 paper.

CHIKI

Design agency: LLdesign
Designer: Lorella Pierdicca
Client: personal work
Date: 2010
Location: Italy

CHIKI is the eco-friendly wrapping cloth, originating from Japanese culture, where care for environment and waste are part of everyday life. Using origami-like techniques, CHIKI can be used as a gift wrapping, a shopping bag, or even a fashion accessory.

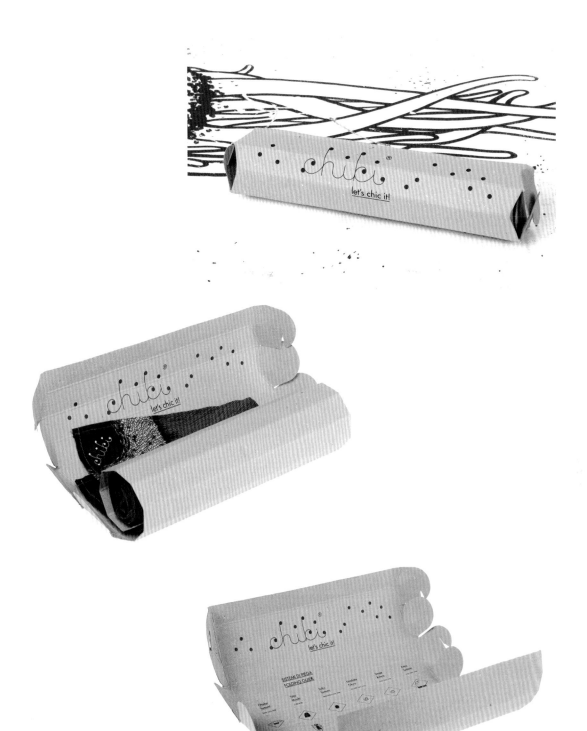

Oh You Really Shouldn't Have!

Design agency: Clairewt
Designer: Claire Ward-Thornton
Client: personal work
Date: 2010
Location: UK

Claire Ward-Thornton is a London based illustrator and designer who has produced a gift wrap that's also a gift. This fun and quirky wrap makes present giving even more special for the people we really care about. Claire Ward-Thornton's project 'Oh you really shouldn't have!' is a limited edition screen print and three dimensional art work which, once unravelled tells the personal story of the gift it once contained… with love in the creases.

Clayboy Wrapping Paper

Design agency: Thenweplay
Designer: Tristan Cruz
Client: Clayboy
Date: 2010
Location: Philippine

Clayboy is an independent craft store located in the heart of Orange County specialising in ceramic art and letterpress.Thenweplay had the privilege to create some really dynamic promotional pieces inspired directly from the founders. Thenweplay's goal was to convey the quirky personalities of the client, however, made sure that the design was very clean and inviting without veering to far from the core brand. The end results was an illustration of both of the founders and their lovely dog. The wrapping paper is now used as promotional gift wraps for customers who visit the store.

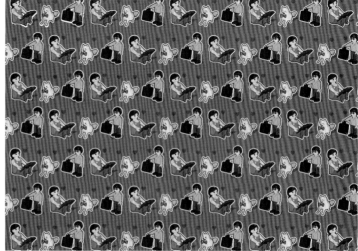

Design agency: In-House Creative Team
Designer: Derek John Dudek
Client: Bravo TV
Date: 2009
Location: USA

It is custom wrapping designed for the ad sales team for holiday client giveaways. Large presence branded with the signature Bravo TV talk bubbles.

Hand Drawn Kraft Wrapping Paper

Designer: Kellie Dykast
Client: personal work
Date: 2011
Location: USA

Using standard kraft paper that is used for shipping packages, designs were hand drawn using a silver paint pen. After the designs were drawn, gifts were wrapped up then tied with red yarn. Next the fabric tags were attached and the names were drawn directly onto the fabric using a black marker.

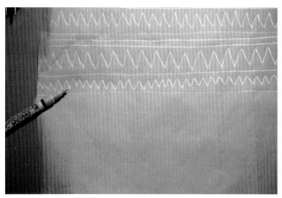

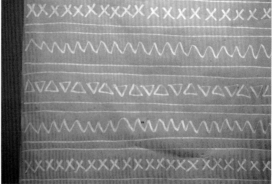

Design agency: I Like Yellow
Designer: Eleftheria Alexandri
Client: personal work
Date: 2009
Location: Greece

A set of three circus-inspired wrapping papers was created for the unexpected thrill of a gift. The start-up idea was to maintain a contemporary look that expresses pleasure and enjoyment while revisiting a childhood fascination. Rendered with clean lines and a retro palette the illustrations blend playfully modern and vintage styles, while the themes developed from the fun circus repertoire of acrobat and animal acts. With the addition of some whimsical elements just to spice things up, the result is joyful and magical.

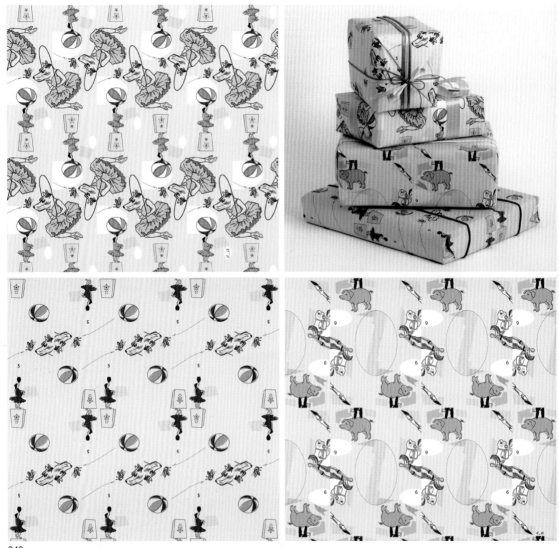

Holiday Gift Wrapping Paper

Design agency: KAA Design Group, Inc.
Designer: Christina Cheng, Annette Lee, Alicia Nagel, Louis-Philippe
         Carretta
Client: KAA Design Group, Inc.
Date: 2007
Location: USA

This holiday gift wrapping paper set comes with four different pattern designs along with tags and ribbons. Both front and back can be used. Each design can be mixed and matched with each other to maximise the users' creative level.

Christmas Gift Box

Design agency: Politanski Design
Designer: Tomasz Politanski
Client: MADE IN LODZ
Date: 2009
Location: Poland

The client commissioned the office to design an
original packaging for a symbolic Christmas gift in
the form of a paper star, offered by the agency to its
clients. Politanski Design decided to enclose the gift in
a cubical box, focusing on structuring it in a manner
that enabled its opening and reaching for the gift with
just one touch of the hand.

Personal Paper

Designer: Stine Engels Henriksen
Client: personal work
Date: 2012
Location: Denmark

An easy way to personalise your wrapping is to make your own pattern
on the wrapping paper. Because the patterns are hand drawn it will give
your gifts a unique look. The best thing is you do not have to be great at
drawing even simple shapes will work.

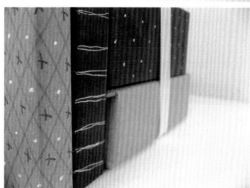

Design agency: Turnstyle
Designer: Madeleine Eiche
Client: Hemlock Printers
Date: 2010
Location: USA

This gift wrap—complete with box and gift tags—was designed for Hemlock Printers as a holiday promotion. Each sheet of wrapping paper is double-sided and there are eight unique designs in all. Hemlock was kind enough to customise a set for Turnstyle to give away to friends as well. What better way to celebrate packages of all shapes and sizes, than with happy wrap to shroud them in joyous anticipation of holiday gift giving.

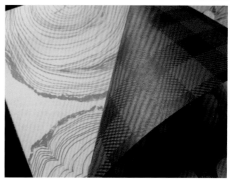

Trima Wish You a Merry Christmas

Design agency: Itziar San Vicente
Designer: Itziar San Vicente
Client: TRIMA
Date: 2010
Location: Spain

TRIMA, a real state agency, had just landed in Madrid and they wanted to communicate its work place in Picasso Tower, Madrid, while wishing a Merry Christmas. The gift packaging contained Gorrotxategi sweets, a traditional vasque product and a Christmas card. The guidelines where to create something informative but cool and casual.

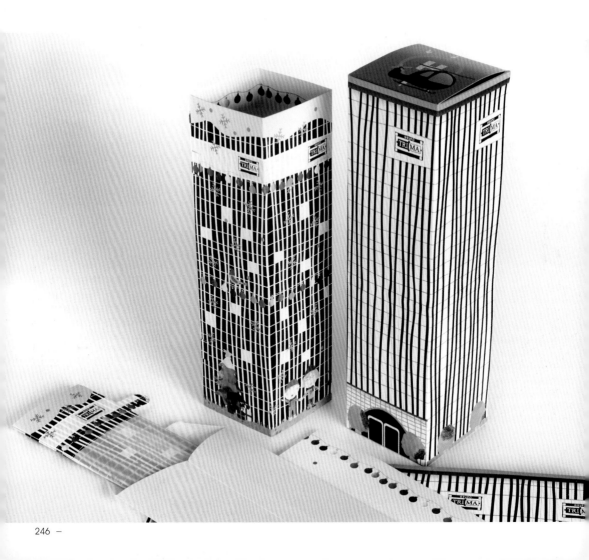

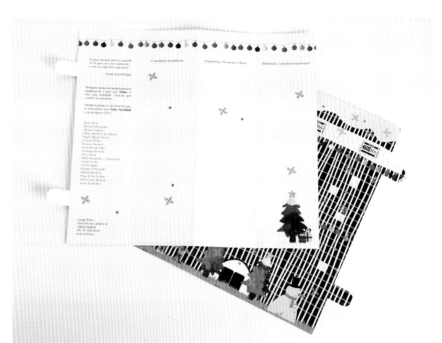

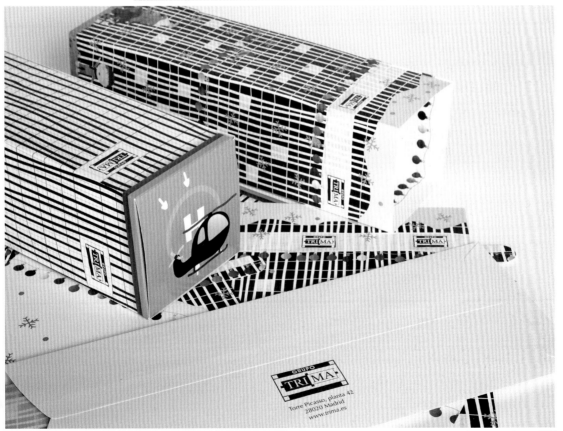

Penhaligon's Christmas Gift Collection 2010

Design agency: jkr
Designer: Sakiko Kobayashi
Client: Penhaligon's
Date: 2010
Location: UK

The design creates a fantasy world communicating the whimsical nature of the brand. Each range transports the receiver into an imaginary place where rabbits attend afternoon tea parties and play musical instruments. Decadence is delivered through the sumptuous patterns, materials and finishes while the rich velvet carry handles provide the finishing touch.

Penhaligon's Christmas Gift Collection 2011

Design agency: jkr
Designer: Sarah Harvey
Client: Penhaligon's
Date: 2011
Location: UK

The theme of 'Hidden London' was chosen as a way to express the
eccentric nature of the Penhaligon's brand. Each gift box provides a
glimpse into life in a Victorian household, with three boxes stacking up to
display a six-storey house. While one side shows the exterior of the house,
inspired by the brand's Covent Garden store, the other 3 faces take you
indoors to explore the madness of an English household at that time.

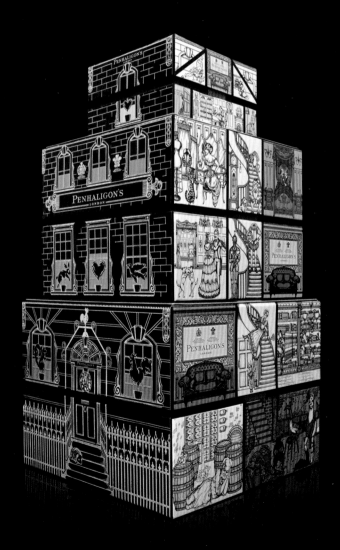

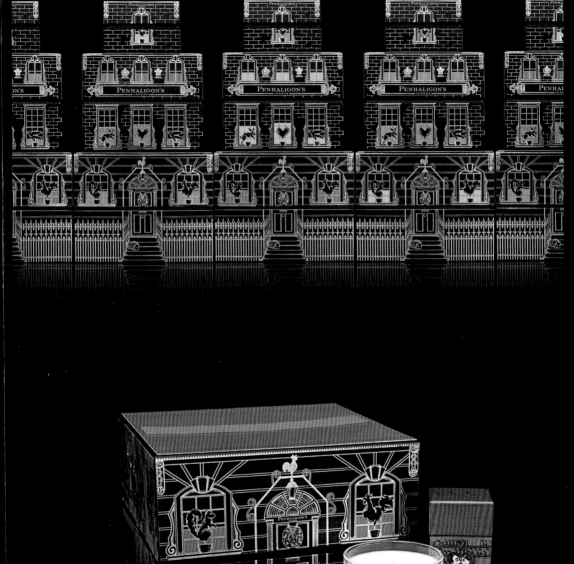

Flower Gift Boxes

Design agency: Iowa State University
Designer: Katie Munn, Erica Wilson
Client: personal work
Date: 2011
Location: USA

These unique and customisable Flower Gift Boxes give customers the option of choosing just the right size, pattern, and colour combination for their gifts. The flowers and bases were constructed using Origami folding techniques and each pattern was created by the designers. Materials used were paper and pearl beads. These gift boxes are gifts in and of themselves.

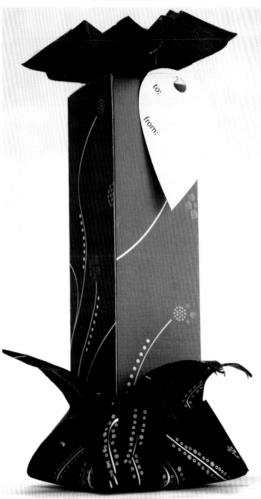

Christmas Wrap Kit

Design agency: No-zebra
Designer: Anja Rustemeier Katie Munn, Erica Wilson
Client: dawanda.com
Date: 2010
Location: Germany

Make your Christmas Gifts look nice and charming! This Christmas Wrap Kit comes with different kinds of cards and stickers which fit perfectly to the cans made of brushed metal. The cards (70mm x 28mm) are printed on 300g paper, matt laminated and have a writable backside, while the stickers (22mm x 22mm) are printed on a glossy vinyl. The cans are made of brushed metal and have a transparent cap.

Handmade Christmas Boxes

Designer: Romina Iannuzzi
Client: personal work
Date: 2009
Location: Germany

Create a design for your gift box, print it out, cut and stick, buy something
to put inside, close with a name tag, give the present to the person you
made it for... done!

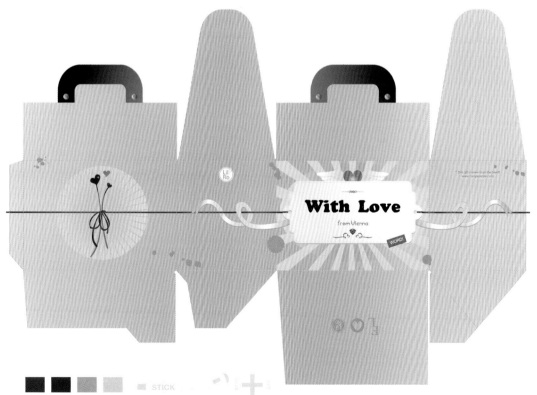

Holiday Fan Wrap

Design agency: Shiho Masuda Style and Design
Designer: Shiho Masuda
Client: Chopsticks NY Magazine
Date: 2011
Location: Japan

It was designed and created for a magazine article in Chopsticks NY's holiday issue, 'Infuse A Japanese Essence Into Your Gift Wrappings.' This package was created with decorative papers and sheer gold ribbon with a holiday ornament. The design was shown with step-by-step instructions for an inspiration of holiday wrapping.

Shirt Style Wrap

Design agency: Shiho Masuda Style and Design
Designer: Shiho Masuda
Client: Lee's Art Shop
Date: 2010
Location: USA

It was designed and created for Lee's Art Shop in Manhattan for their in-store display of holiday custom gift packaging. The paper used for this gift wrapping is a mat-finished washi paper with a Japanese print pattern. Pleated gold paper is used as an accent for centre of the package. Black satin ribbon creates a neck tie as a fashionable accessory. The design became popular for custom packaging orders and entertained many New Yorkers.

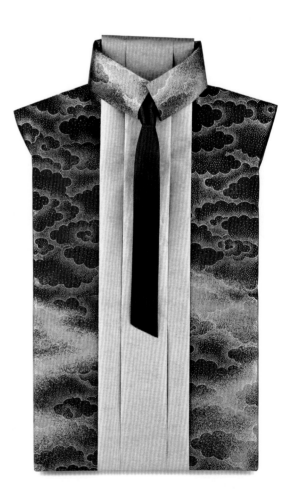

Dotty

Design agency: Sophia Victoria Joy
Designer: Sophia Victoria Joy
Client: Sophia Victoria Joy
Date: 2012
Location: UK

It is inspired by quirky tea shops, gorgeous delicatessens and the smell of fresh coffee. The Dotty gift wrap is a spotty delight. Hand screen printed onto luxury 100% recycled brown paper. This gift wrap is British quality at its best. It is brilliant for use all year round. Match the Dotty and Love Hearts mint gift tags with ribbon bobbins and string bobbins for a brilliant finish. Gift wrap measures 50cm x 70 cm.

Love Birds

Design agency: Sophia Victoria Joy
Designer: Sophia Victoria Joy
Client: Sophia Victoria Joy
Date: 2012
Location: UK

This gift wrap is perfect for any celebration throughout the year and features a bright and beautiful flock of doves carrying ribbons and horse shoes in their beaks. This is ideal for birthdays, weddings, christenings, romantic celebrations or a thank you gift. Screen printed onto 100% recycled luxury white kraft paper. It is available in violet, aqua and fuschia. Gift wrap measures 50cm x 70 cm.

Keep Cosy This Christmas

Design agency: Sophia Victoria Joy
Designer: Sophia Victoria Joy
Client: Sophia Victoria Joy
Date: 2012
Location: UK

We love keeping cosy at Christmas! Piling the knitwear on and snuggling by the fire, with a nice cup of tea! This wrapping paper was inspired by just that. Each quirky woolly hat was filled with intricate patterns, inspired by vintage knitwear. With 'Keep Cosy This Christmas' hand screen printed in a bold traditional font, this gift wrap was filled with character. Hand screen printed onto 100% recycled luxury brown kraft paper. Each sheet is printed using eco friendly water based inks. Gift wrap measures 50cm x 70 cm.

Love Hearts

Design agency: Sophia Victoria Joy
Designer: Sophia Victoria Joy
Client: Sophia Victoria Joy
Date: 2012
Location: UK

This gorgeous gift wrap features Sophia Victoria Joy's best-selling love heart design hand screen printed onto luxury 100% recycled rustic brown or white paper. This gift wrap is high quality and designed and created in Britain. Pretty patterns fill the hearts across the traditional brown paper to add a truly special finish to any gift. Gift wrap measures 50cm x 70 cm.

Blooming Paper

Designer: Stine Engels Henriksen
Client: personal work
Date: 2011
Location: Denmark

Stine Engels Henriksen wanted to wrap these gifts in a way that made them look lush, fun and almost over the top, but he also wanted to use simple, inexpensive materials. The designer rolled a lot of small cones out of brightly coloured notepaper and stuck them together as petals creating flowers.

Shop-Gift-Wrapping

Design agency: Atelier Ace
Designer: Belin Liu
Client: Ace Hotel
Date: 2011
Location: USA

Silkscreened, black-striped kraft gift wrapping paper with jute rope and a custom gift tag were exclusively made for the Ace Hotel Shop (shop.acehotel.com). A special message hand-printed onto paper ephemera culled from vintage National Geographics, encyclopedia books and Arizona Highways magazines was also included.

Design agency: Zentoweb
Designer: Viktoria Kletsko
Client: Vintage Christmas
Date: 2011
Location: Germany

The main idea was to create a Christmas mood without any traditional elements like snowflakes, Santa, the Christmas tree and so on. The package must convey a small sign of the of the present inside. The red craft paper with the pack thread indicating your present has come from far away. The golden bird from the seal has brought it especially for you. The red craft paper with a stripy button – don't you expect to find something chic or at least unusual inside? What does the rice wrapping paper with a Chinese stamp hide? Of course, you cannot overlook the same striped button, so you understand immediately that this present is also for you! The walls of the office or the house are already decked with Christmas decorations and branches, so try to avoid piling them up on your gift packaging too.

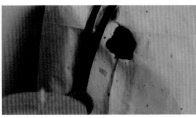

Designer: Stine Engels Henriksen
Client: personal work
Date: 2012
Location: Denmark

Instead of throwing out away your worn out jeans use them to wrap your gifts. Fabrics are perfect for gift wrapping and easy to decorate with embroidery, drawings or beads.

Designer: Stine Engels Henriksen
Client: Personal work
Date: 2011
Location: Denmark

It is often the right combination of materials that make a gift look great rather than the cost of the materials. Here recycled paper used as cushioning from a package the designer received, combined with classic red/white cotton string and pieces of natural materials found in the midst of Danish winter.

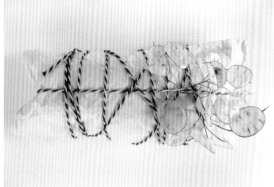

Design agency: Studio Kudos
Client: Studio Kudos
Date: 2009
Location: USA

Large circular and starbursts graphics created from the number nine and ten, were rendered in fluorescent green and metallic bronze. Pop Pop is part of the holiday gifting tradition started in 2008, featuring two large numbers taken from the last digit of the current year and the following. Each year Studio Kudos picks two contrasting colours and creates patterns from basic geometric shapes. When viewed from a distance one can see the large numbers, however they make great randomized patterns when wrapped around objects of various size and shape.

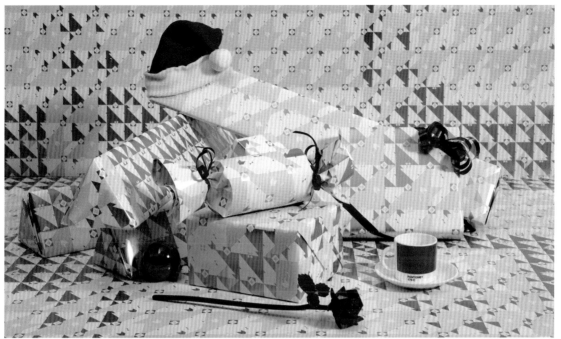

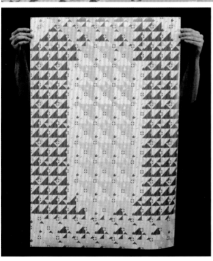

Pyramid Party

Design agency: Studio Kudos
Client: Studio Kudos
Date: 2009
Location: USA

Large triangular graphics created from the number zero and one, were rendered in fluorescent yellow and metallic purple. Pyramid Party is part of the holiday gifting tradition started in 2008, featuring two large numbers taken from the last digit of the current year and the following.

Gift for Christmas 2009

Design agency: Zoo Studio
Designer: Xavier Castells
Client: Zoo Studio
Date: 2009
Location: Spain

The packaging was designed for Christmas promotional gift.

INDEX

Katy Verbrugge	Rachel Brinkman
Kellie Dykast	REB Design
Keri Thornton	Rob Ryan
Kristy Jean Design	Romina Iannuzzi
La Tigre	RR Donnelley Ireland
LLdesign	Savannah College of Art and Design
Luisa Arango	Shiho Masuda Style and Design
Manic	SicolaMartin
Marin Santic	Sid Lee
Marina Androsovich	Sophia Georgopoulou
MarmeladStudio	Sophia Victoria Joy
Matter Strategic Design	SPECTRO DESIGN STUDIO
Mediacrat	Stine Engels Henriksen
Mei Yan Lau	Studio Baklazan
Michelle Gray	Studio Kmzero
Misako Ishida	Studio Kudos
Morgan Agency	Studio Móbi
MOZAIQ eco design	The Getz
Néstor Silvosa	The Inklings of Tess
nhouse studio V&D	The Savannah College of Art and Design
Nicolai Henriksen, Thorbjørn Gudnason, Christina Stougaard, Casper Holden	Thenweplay
Nikki Gittins Design	Thisismaurix
Northink	Tiana Avila Design
No-zebra	To Be Designed Co., Ltd
Olle Sundin	Turnstyle
p576	Vasily KasSab
Petek Design	Victor Branding Design Corp
Pik Chu Ahmetaj	WitShop
Pixels Plus Paper	Yana Stepchenko
Politanski Design	Zoo Studio
	zweizueins

©2013 by Design Media Publishing Limited
This edition published in September 2013

Design Media Publishing Limited
20/F Manulife Tower
169 Electric Rd, North Point
Hong Kong
Tel: 00852-28672587
Fax: 00852-25050411
E-mail: suisusie@gmail.com
www.designmediahk.com

Editing: Amone Hsieh, Kristy Wen Ho
Proofreading: YIN Qian
Design/Layout: ZHOU Jie, LU Haoyang

ISBN 978-988-15451-1-4

Printed in China